# LIFE PARABLES

# LIFE PARABLES

discovering god's extraordinary truths in life's ordinary moments

Brad Nelson

ISBN: 0692725423
ISBN 13: 9780692725429

*Dedicated to the love of my life, Kerrie,*
*and my two incredible children, Drew and Abby!*

## Acknowledgements

Attempting to thank large groups of people can be a dangerous endeavor because you will inevitably forget someone who deserves your appreciation. That said I felt compelled to mention several individuals who played a role in this book making it to print. It has been a long and arduous task and without the help and support of these beautiful people I never would have made it.

First and foremost I thank my Lord and Savior Jesus Christ. This is not a cliché statement. Jesus is everything to me and without him I would be nothing. It is because of him and for him that this book has been written. My prayer is for this book to bring him much glory.

Thanks to my lovely wife, Kerrie, who has believed in me throughout this process.

Thanks to my kids, Drew and Abby, for being a continual source of life parables. Keep them coming!

Thanks to my parents, Gary and Peggy, for all your prayers and encouragement throughout my life.

Thanks to those who encouraged me in my writing along the way: Tim Clawson, Natalie Shelpuk, Anand family, Meiers family and Jacinda Munise.

Thank you to my proof-readers: Susan Kennedy, Kerrie Nelson, and Dennis Cone. You guys make me look good! People actually think I know how to spell and punctuate.

A special thank you to my pastor and friend, Peter Nugent, who allowed me to take time each week away from my duties at the church to write. The guidance you've provided throughout this process has been invaluable.

I'm grateful to my church families at Princeton Bible Church and Grace Baptist Church. It has been an absolute honor to minister alongside you for all these years. Thanks for your prayers!

# Contents

# Forward

Almost 20 years ago, I sat among a group of adults and teens at a summer youth camp as Pastor Brad Nelson used his life experiences to explain biblical truths in a way that everyone could relate to. The entire audience was captivated, and came away with a deeper awareness and appreciation of the presence and power of God in our lives. That camp in southern Missouri impacted our lives forever. Even today, twenty years later, when I run into someone that was at that camp, we always end up reminiscing about what God did in our lives that week.

That was the beginning of a long and precious relationship with Brad and his family. Brad was senior pastor of Princeton Bible Church in New Jersey. I am a pastor in Lees Summit, MO. Every year, Brad and his wife, Kerrie, came back to the Midwest as the guest speaker at our summer teen camp. Each and every year, Brad connected with the students and counselors with wonderful tales from his life, which in turn, connected them with God in some way.

I am privileged to introduce to you "Life's Parables", a collection of anecdotes from Brad's life that are sure to resonate with you. Each of these modern day parables contains timeless biblical truths set in the 21st century.

You will laugh as you read about the time that Brad bought his new bride a microwave cart. You will find strength as you read about Brad's son facing his biggest fear. You will find hope as read how what seems to be the worst of times of our lives become some of the best moments in our lives. Each chapter contains an occasion in Brad's life that God revealed Himself in a powerful way. Each chapter will help you to discover God's handiwork in your own life.

Brad has had a significant impact on my life, and the lives of hundreds of people through his practical teaching and impactful preaching. I am sure that this book will be just as helpful in your life as well.

God Bless,
Pastor Peter Nugent

# Introduction

I vividly remember as a kid wanting to be part of the adult group at all our family gatherings. Whenever we would celebrate holidays or special occasions together, I didn't want to be stuck at the kiddie table! I wanted to be where the action was. My desire to be around my aunts, uncles, grandparents, and parents wasn't driven by some youthful longing to be older. I just loved hearing their stories! Storytelling at our family gatherings was inevitable. The adults would be gathered around in the living room or outside on the patio, chit-chatting about the routine happenings of life. A random comment from someone in the group would prime the pump and cause another to say, "Remember when . . . ?" or "I remember the time. . . " Then the floodgates would open, and everyone would start sharing life stories that had been indelibly etched in their minds. They would even request certain stories, "Hey, Mom, tell the one about the time . . . !" It didn't matter if the story had been told dozens of times before. Their enthusiasm was the same whether they were telling the story for the first time or the hundredth time. The audience hung on every word even though they probably knew the story better than the one telling it. They would laugh. They would cry. More than anything they would remember the lessons they had learned. The events shared in those stories had shaped their lives, and they looked back on them with a deep fondness. It was these stories and their lessons that played a major role in plotting the course of their lives. To this day I still love to be in a room with my parents and their siblings when they start sharing life stories. I didn't realize it during the years of my youth, but listening to the stories of my elders had a huge impact on my life as well. That's the thing about stories—they not only shape us, but they impact those who are privileged enough to listen.

Everyone has a story to tell! In fact, our lives are a series of stories or parables. Some are short. Some are epic. Some are funny. Some are tragic. Some delight our souls. Some cast us into the depths of despair. Most involve mundane aspects of everyday life, but some include rare, extraordinary adventures. Distracted by the affairs of life, we often blow past these stories—and the truths they contain—without giving them a second thought. We rarely pause to consider that God is trying to speak to us through the ordinary activities of life. Can God really speak to us through a routine trip to the doctor? Can He really use a hamster to teach us a life-changing principle about time management? Will God make Himself known to us though a microwave cart? Yes! Yes! And yes!

God is the Author of your life. The stories of your life are unfolding according to His divine script. Everything that happens to you and around you happens for a reason. God is continually attempting to instruct, to communicate, and to change us through all the events of our lives. He wants to leverage these events, in concert with His word, to make us more like our Savior, Jesus Christ. As recorded in Scripture, Jesus used things such as seeds, farmers, dirt, birds, treasure, judges, friends, leaven, wheat, weeds, pearls, fish, sheep, coins, vineyards, and weddings to teach mankind some of the most profound biblical truths we've ever heard. Why do we think God can't do the same in our lives as we go through the ordinary activities of our days? *Life's ordinary events contain God's extraordinary lessons.*

God understands humans better than we understand ourselves. He recognizes the things that get our attention. He knows how we learn best. Obviously, God's Word (the Bible) is the primary vehicle God uses to speak into our lives, but He also uses the physical creation and the circumstances of our lives to teach us. God knows that we learn best when we have a physical example to observe. When the truths of God's Word intersect with the circumstances of life, something special happens, and we're able to grasp spiritual principles that will stay with us for the rest of our natural lives. They become the stories that we'll share at family gatherings and with anyone else who will listen. These life stories become one of the tools God uses to build godly character in us.

I've been a Christ follower for more than twenty-six years and have been through a great number of adventures with Him along the way. Over that time I've read the Bible repeatedly. I've studied the Bible for years. I've learned innumerable facts about God and Jesus. But there have been only a handful of moments when God's Word came alive through the circumstances of life, and He taught me principles that literally changed my life. These are truths that shaped the course of my life and ministry. A few years ago God impressed on my heart to write down my stories in a book for the purpose of helping other Christ followers. I want to invite you into my family gathering as I share a few of the parables of my life, times when God took a physical occurrence and used it to teach me a great spiritual principle. Hopefully, my stories will encourage you to pay attention and consider what God is trying to teach you through the parables of your life.

# 1

## The Half-Dead Life

***Allowing God to open our eyes to a world filled with people in need.***

Ah! The Big Apple in July—hot, muggy, and crowded. The cavernous streets of Time Square are buzzing with activity. Tourists trip over themselves as they walk with heads tilted skyward in hopes of catching a glimpse of the tops of the skyscrapers. A group of ladies stop to have their picture taken with the Naked Cowboy. Thousands of people wait in line at the "Tickets, Tickets" booth hoping to acquire tickets to the latest Broadway smash hit. Street vendors hawk their wares to an unsuspecting tourist who is trying to figure out how a movie still in the theaters could already be on DVD. Native New Yorkers hurriedly pass by with music blaring through their earphones and contempt in their eyes for the crowds that are making it even more difficult for them to get to work on time.

All in all, it's a fairly typical Saturday afternoon in New York City with one exception—a street fair that stretches up Broadway from Forty-second Street to Fifty-seventh Street. The street fair takes the classic NYC excitement to a whole new level. Merchants from all five boroughs have descended on Manhattan and are peddling their goods to us as we slowly make our way through the sea of people. I'm with my wife, Kerrie, so we pause frequently to look at cheap sunglasses, fruit, and fake Gucci bags. Finally, we reach Fifty-seventh Street and turn west toward our hotel. The crowd begins to thin as we make our way toward a night of luxury and celebration of our wedding anniversary. It's going to be a night to remember—dinner at a little Italian restaurant, a hit Broadway play my wife has always wanted to see, a late-evening stroll through streets of Manhattan, and a night of extravagance spent in an upscale hotel near Central Park. With our hotel in sight I notice something lying on the sidewalk just ahead of us. As we draw nearer to the dark mass, I realize it's not something, but someone!

His face is soiled and weathered from too many days and nights spent out in the elements. The creases and lines in his face are like the cracks and seams in the sidewalk. His clothes are filthy and torn and reek of sweat. He lies spread eagle on a bed of trash bags, which I assume contain his most prized possessions—his only possessions. His eyes are closed, his chapped lips gape wide open, and he's not moving. Is he breathing? Could he be dead? Passed out most likely—malnourished, drunk, stoned, sleep-deprived. This nameless man is lying half-dead on a sidewalk in one of the most populous cities in the world as hundreds of people (me included) walk around him or step over him without giving it a second thought. They have become numb to his existence. They justify their apathy by considering their own difficulties, by demeaning the impact of any effort they might make, or by casting judgment on the man—he got what he deserved.

As I pause at the next intersection I glance with tear-filled eyes back over my shoulder toward the half-dead man. I wish I could do something substantial to help this man but I've got big plans for the evening. It's our twentieth wedding anniversary after all. We only have one night in the city. We have hotel reservations, dinner reservations, and a Broadway play to experience. Surely someone else, somebody who isn't celebrating their anniversary, who isn't so busy, will come along and do something to help out this poor soul. I hope so! I say a quick prayer that God will send someone to come and tend to the needs of this half-dead man—never considering that I was the answer to my own prayer.

I did my best to delete this experience from my memory banks, but throughout dinner, the play, and our stroll on the busy streets of Manhattan, I found it increasingly difficult to put the half-dead man out of my mind.

His face, his smell, and his lifeless body, coupled with my own failure to act, were haunting me. As if that weren't enough, God was also troubling me by bringing Scripture to my mind. I was struck by the eerie similarities between what I had just experienced and a story Jesus told about another half-dead man and a trio of people who had an opportunity to help him out.

"A certain man went down from Jerusalem to Jericho, and fell among thieves, which stripped him of his raiment, and wounded him, and departed, leaving him half dead" (Luke 10:30). He's most likely a business man of some sort who ends up in the wrong place at the wrong time. After a week of business in Jerusalem, he's tired and ready to make the seventeen-mile trek back home to Jericho. As he sets out on his journey, he's undoubtedly a little nervous because parts of this road have become known as the "way of blood." But he calms his nerves by telling himself he's made this journey numerous times with no problems. Without warning, his thoughts of home are interrupted, and he finds himself surrounded by a gang of mindless thugs. His mind races, "This is not good! There are too many to fight. There's no way I can outrun them all with my bad knee. To call for help would only provoke them. What should I do? Reason. That's it, reason with them." That seems like the best option. His pleas for mercy and compassion are met with laughter and ridicule. Without provocation the leader of the gang is now in his face demanding he hand over all his money and they'll think about sparing his life. He starts to open his mouth in protest when suddenly his whole world goes black as a large rock slams into the back of his skull. Even though he's unconscious, the thieves continue to kick and punch the man as blood begins to pour from his mouth, nose, and ears. Just like that nameless half-dead homeless person in NYC, the man in Jesus' story is hurting, has suffered loss, and been left for dead by the side of the road. The gang rifles through his bags and begins to strip him of his garments. It's not their biggest score ever, but they're pleased with their haul for the day. The gang quickly flees the scene of the crime as they hear someone else coming down the road from the opposite direction.

*THE PRIEST*

A few moments later someone comes around the corner and sees the crumpled mass by the side of the road. This is no ordinary "someone"; he's a Jewish priest. He pauses for a moment as he tries to make out the shape of what he thinks might be a human being. It's the half-dead man's lucky day! As chance would have it, he has been discovered very quickly by a man who has dedicated his life to serving God. The priest of Israel is highly educated, influential, and well respected in the community. He's the representative of God on earth for the Jewish people. He's the one who shows people how to live in accordance with God's principles. He knows Scripture incredibly well and is charged with helping others to live by God's Word. For these reasons his response to this situation is somewhat perplexing. Jesus said, "And when he saw him, he passed by on the other side" (Luke 10:31) He does what? After discerning that this is in fact a half-dead man, the priest intentionally walks way around him on the other side of the road. He pretends he doesn't notice the man as he looks the other direction, whistling his favorite hymn. Judgmental and condescending thoughts race through his mind as he tries to justify his unwillingness to help a person in need: "Dirty sinner! He got what he deserved. Serves him right for traveling this dangerous road all alone."

He doesn't want to be inconvenienced with this man's problem any more than he has been already by having to move to the other side of the road. After all, he's an important and busy man with places to go and people to see. He doesn't want to get involved because that could throw off his very busy schedule, not to mention what will happen if the man turns out to be dead or dies in the process of his helping. If he happens to be dead and the priest touches him, he will be defiled according to the Jewish law. He certainly doesn't need that kind of hassle. And besides, even if he's not dead, the chances are he's going to die anyway, so why bother? Buzzards have to eat too. No, the best policy for this sanctimonious man is to not get involved but mind his own business. He's going to stick to his much more sterile plan of self-righteousness, judgment, and denial.

### *THE LEVITE*

As the half-dead man struggles to regain consciousness, he senses someone standing over him. It's all he can do to narrowly open his eyes. Against the scorching Middle Eastern sun he makes out the silhouette of a man dressed in traditional Levitical garments. Like a vapor the man is gone. Was it a dream? Was his head injury causing him to hallucinate? As he contemplates the reality of his potential savior, he once again slips into unconsciousness.

The half-dead man wasn't dreaming or hallucinating. He, in fact, did see a Levite standing over him. Luke records it this way: "And likewise a Levite, when he was at the place, came and looked on him, and passed by on the other side" (10:32). A second passerby, who we'll call the sympathetic man, is from the tribe of Levi, the priestly tribe. He's undoubtedly very religious and serves God faithfully as he carries out his responsibilities in the temple at Jerusalem. As he strolls down the road asking God to help him fulfill his ministry responsibilities, he notices a naked figure in the ditch by the side of the road. His mind begins to race, "Oh my! What should I do?" He tentatively makes his way over to the figure. "Is he alive?" he thinks. At that moment the figure groans, startling the Levite. The sympathetic man makes his way around to the front of the man so he can get a look at his face. He feels so bad for him. He wonders to himself, "Who would do such a thing to someone?" As he gazes tearfully into the face of the half-dead man, he notices the eyes start to open, and his mind immediately kicks into overdrive as he weighs his options. "I've got to be at the temple by 5:00 p.m. to carry out my annual ministry duties. This guy is half-dead and in need of some serious medical attention—I'm no doctor. He can't walk and who knows how long it will take me to carry him to the nearest place where he can receive attention? Not only that, how will I pay? I don't have two shekels to rub together. What if the thieves are still nearby? What if they're waiting to spring their lethal trap on me? I feel bad for the guy, but I have my own problems!" He comes to the conclusion that any efforts he would make would be minuscule and most likely in vain. His feelings of sympathy for the man's situation aren't enough to spur him to action. He feels bad and sheds a tear, but after all is said and done, he leaves the man to die and passes by on the other side of the road.

### *THE SAMARITAN*

The Samaritans were a shunned group of half-Jewish, half-Gentile people who were despised and looked down on by the full-blooded Jewish people. Interaction between the Jews and the Samaritans was, for the most part, nonexistent. In a Jew's mind a Samaritan was a second class citizen, and it's safe to say that Samaritans had no great love for the Jews either. Given this information, what do you expect the response to be when a Samaritan comes across a half-dead Jewish man in need of assistance? A cold, callous heart filled with anger that ignores the need and passes by on the other side of the road. But what do we see in Jesus' story? The exact opposite.

"But a certain Samaritan, as he journeyed, came where he was: and when he saw him, he had compassion on him, and went to him, and bound up his wounds, pouring in oil and wine, and set him on his own beast, and brought him to an inn, and took care of him. And on the morrow when he departed, he took out two pence, and gave them to the host, and said unto him, Take care of him; and whatsoever thou spendest more, when I come again, I will repay thee" (10:33–35). The Samaritan has most likely traveled this road hundreds of times before on his way to conduct business in the nearby villages of the region. He's on a journey. His time is precious and his calendar full. He has things to do and people to meet. But a person in need, even if he's Jewish, is more important than his schedule. Like the previous two passersby, the Samaritan man notices the half-dead man as he makes his way along this road. However, his response is drastically different. He takes action. He goes to him and assesses his condition. He doesn't pass by on the other side of the road. He doesn't feel bad for the guy from a distance. He gets involved. He goes right to where the person is hurting, into the dirt and blood, and starts to bind up his wounds the best he knows how with the resources he has at his disposal. He does what he can to help, and it costs him. He uses his oil, his wine; he lets the guy ride on his beast; he pays for his hotel room and medical attention; he stays all night with him in the hotel room and tends to his wounds. He follows up to make sure the guy is OK and that there are no additional expenses that need to be covered. It's safe to say the Samaritan was more than a little inconvenienced as a result of helping the half-dead stranger. In all this don't lose sight of the fact he doesn't know this guy at all. In fact, it wouldn't be a stretch to say they would consider one another enemies. That's what makes his actions even more remarkable!

The Samaritan man is not worried about being taken advantage of or about his own personal welfare. He wants to help this person recover from his pain. In order to do that, he has to participate in his pain. Helping half-dead people is hard, dirty, costly work, but the payoff is huge. Whereas the first two guys thought, "What will happen to us if we help?" The Samaritan man thought, "What will happen to this man if I don't help?" The Samaritan man sees the situation, and his compassion compels him to get involved. This is greater than the sympathy felt by the previous passerby, who sheds a tear and passes by on the other side of the road. It's an intense inward emotion that drives him to action. For him there's no other option; he has to help regardless of the personal costs or inconvenience.

## WHO ARE YOU?

This is one of the most famous parables ever told by Jesus. If you grew up in church, you have no doubt heard this story multiple times. Even if you are from a non-church background, you know the phrase "good Samaritan." But let me ask you a question that will hopefully make this story a bit more personal. Of all the characters in Jesus' story, who are you? To which character do you relate the most? Are you one of the thieves?

### *THE THIEVES*

You forgot about them, didn't you? They're the ones that caused the problem in the first place. The thief is a user and an abuser. He views people as objects and nothing more than a means to an end. He gives no thought to how his actions might hurt or even destroy other people. He is a steamroller, whose only concern is for self. Don't be too quick to dismiss the notion that you might be the thief in this story. From time to time we've all probably been guilty of robbing others in one sense. Maybe we would never dream of robbing someone at gunpoint or physically accosting someone, but have we robbed them emotionally with our words? Have we stolen glory from another? Have we trampled on the feelings of someone as we told a joke at their expense? Have you cut people with your words and left them emotionally bloodied? In the final analysis, the thief isn't really that different from the priest and the Levite. All three are concerned primarily with one thing—self. Their existence is defined by self-preservation. There's little to no concern for how their actions might impact another person or group of people.

John 10:10 describes the actions of a thief as stealing, killing, and destroying. On a daily basis we see examples of those three things being done to people physically, but I think the more common occurrence is for us to steal, kill, and destroy one another emotionally, relationally, and spiritually. A thief steals someone's virginity for a few moments of personal pleasure. A thief kills someone's hopes and dreams with an unwillingness to support them in their endeavors. A thief destroys a person's self-confidence through a continual barrage of demeaning words. Are you one of the thieves? God is calling you to a new way of doing life. Put away your life of stealing, killing, and destroying and begin giving, reviving, and building people up.

### *THE SANCTIMONIOUS MAN*

Are you the sanctimonious priest in Jesus' story—the one who pretends not to see the man and passes by on the other side of the road? Are you a religious person who can't be bothered with issues facing someone in dire need? Has your religion caused you to become judgmental, cold, and callous? This is the eventual end of all religion. Works-based religion causes us to begin viewing our righteous acts as making us superior to those who aren't quite as "spiritual." Our sanctimonious hearts swell with pride and cast judgment on the half-dead people all around us. Though we may never say it aloud, in our hearts we feel the half-dead people are simply getting what they deserve. They're reaping what they've sown. Self-righteousness defines sanctimonious individuals. At the end of it all, they're really no different from the thieves. While they would never dream of physically accosting someone with a weapon, they—like the thieves—have no real concern beyond their own self-interest. They won't stop and stoop to help someone who is in need. If there is no benefit to them, they don't see the need to get involved. Has your relationship with God turned into nothing more than religious rituals that are puffing you up with pride? Has religion robbed you of your compassion toward those in need? As we grow more like Jesus, our hearts should be filled with more compassion, not more piousness. If you find your heart hard toward the half-dead people surrounding you, ask God to soften your heart and give you a fresh perspective toward those in need.

### *THE SYMPATHETIC MAN*

Do you fall into the camp of the Levite who came and looked at the man but then passed by on the other side of the road? That day in NYC I was most definitely guilty of being a sympathetic Levite. I felt bad for the guy. My heart went out to him. I hoped someone would come along and lend him a hand. But at the end of the day, I did nothing. The Levite was a highly religious person who claimed to know and love God. The fact that he stops to at least look at the half-dead man shows he has some concern for his plight. I see his eyes start to well up with tears as he turns and crosses to the other side of the road. He has all the emotion, even the tears, but no action. He has sympathy, but not compassion. What good is sympathy if it doesn't propel us to action?

You're surrounded by half-dead people who could use your help in some way. Maybe they need financial assistance. Maybe they need a word of encouragement. Maybe they just need you to be patient with them when they are having a hard day. Maybe they need you to be bold enough to talk with them about the one who can make them fully alive. A person like the Levite (with a sympathetic heart) is great at justifying his actions or lack thereof. He's always selling his potential impact on the situation drastically short. "What good could I possibly do? I have so little. I'm not a counselor. I'm no evangelist. I'm a nobody!" He passes on by, hoping, even praying, that someone more qualified will come along and minister to the half-dead person. If you find yourself in this category, you have a sensitive heart but need your sensitivity to move you to action. Stop selling yourself, and God, short. Do what you can to help those in need and watch God abundantly bless your meager efforts.

### *THE SAMARITAN*

God's desire is that all His children would display the compassionate heart of the Samaritan. How does He want us to love our neighbor? The way the Samaritan loved the half-dead man. A Samaritan heart moves beyond sympathy to compassion and action. God wants us to get involved in the pain of others, messy as it may be. Acting as the Samaritan involves personal sacrifice and inconvenience. It is placing the needs of another above your personal agenda.

My son has this type of heart. On a family trip to New York City he demonstrated for me what it means to love your neighbor. It was a few days after Christmas, and the city was still crowded with tourists checking out the sights of the Big Apple. Before we caught our train that morning, my father-in-law had given each of the grandkids twenty dollars to spend during their adventure in the city. One grandkid bought an "I love NYC" T-shirt; another purchased a fake Rolex from a guy on the corner; still another bought every food item the street vendors were peddling (pretzels, roasted nuts, and an unidentified meat-like substance). My son, who was seven at the time, couldn't decide what he wanted and still had his money folded neatly in his pocket.

As we started to make our way back to the train station, we happened past a homeless man seated on the sidewalk with a sign that read, "I'm hungry. Please help me." Most of our group made their way around the man, not giving him a second thought, but my son, who was holding my hand, slowed as we passed this half-dead man. He soaked in every word on the cardboard sign. We had taken a few steps past the man when my son looked up at me with tear-filled eyes. I stopped and kneeled down beside him as I asked, "Do you want to help that man?" He nodded his head as a tear rolled down his cheek. We made our way back to the man, and my son pulled his crisp twenty-dollar bill from his pocket and dropped it into a hat the man had sitting in front of him. As my son displayed compassion through personal sacrifice, I felt my own eyes flood with tears, and I wasn't the only one. In that moment the half-dead man looked up at me with tears streaking down his unwashed face. He was genuinely moved by the actions of this seven-year-old good Samaritan.

As we left the man, my son's tears of compassion were replaced with tears of joy because he knew that he had done all he could to help someone in desperate need. No purchased toy or trinket could have given him the joy he was experiencing in that moment. He had participated in the pain of another, and now he was being blessed beyond measure. He wasn't focused on what it had cost him but on what he had gained. He wasn't worried about being taken advantage of but only knew he had taken advantage of the opportunity to minister to someone in need.

## SEEING HALF-DEAD PEOPLE

As you read this chapter, you could have a tendency to think this is a story about helping the homeless, the poor, or the disenfranchised of society. That's not an unreasonable assumption to make. In fact, I think that's a good application for this story. As followers of Jesus, we should be ministering to the poor. We should be helping those who are in great physical need. However, I think the application of this story goes far beyond ministry to the poor or homeless. Let's not lose sight of the reason Jesus is telling this parable—it's an illustration of what it means to love your neighbor. He's trying to help us understand what it means to love people and is encouraging us to love in the way the Samaritan loved the half-dead man. At the end of the story, Jesus says to his audience, "Go, and do thou likewise" (10:37). While we may or may not have daily contact with people living below the poverty line, we do spend the entirety of our lives rubbing shoulders with half-dead people.

Do you remember the Bruce Willis movie *The Sixth Sense*? The movie was really good, but it freaked me out! The creepiest line in the entire movie was when the little boy said, "I see dead people." The little boy had a sixth sense that caused him to see the souls of dead people all around him. Everywhere he went he had contact with people who were stuck between two worlds. Everyone else passed them by without noticing, but he saw them, had conversations with them, and tried to help them. In a totally non-creepy manner, let me say, "I see half-dead people." In Genesis, God tells Adam and Eve that their disobedience to His clear commands will bring an instant penalty of death. However, Scripture says they lived hundreds of years after their fall. What gives? Did God misspeak? Not at all. On the day they sinned, they died spiritually (lost the Spirit of God), but they continued to live in the physical world; they became half-dead people. The people you work with, live next to, or go to soccer games with are all half-dead without Jesus as Savior. They're alive physically, but spiritually they're dead to God. Ephesians 2:1 tells us that in Christ we have been made alive though once we were dead.

As a result of our sinfulness, this world is a broken and hurting place. We are surrounded by people who are hurting—people who have been used and abused and thrown out like garbage, who feel unloved, unwanted, half-dead. On the outside, they may appear to have it all together, but when you come to where they are and get involved in their lives, you come to realize how desperate their situation really is. Do you even notice them anymore, or do you simply step over them and continue on with your life, pretending everything is OK? At the end of this story Jesus gives us our marching orders. He says, "Go and do likewise." We, like the Samaritan man, can help them. We have the resources at our disposal to bring about change and make half-life into abundant life. We need God to fill our hearts with compassion for these people, so that we can move beyond the fear and selfishness and begin living a Samaritan-like life.

### *THE HALF-DEAD MAN*

Earlier I asked you who you were in Jesus' story—the thieves, the priest, the Levite, or the Samaritan. But there is one character in the story I want to revisit—the half-dead man. Maybe as you're reading this, you find yourself relating to the man left for dead on the side of the road. You feel used and abused by the world. You feel abandoned by those you thought loved you. You wonder if anyone will ever come to your aid. To a certain extent, we've all been the half-dead man at some point in our life. At the very least we can all relate to his condition in a spiritual sense. All of us, while alive physically, were at some point, or still are, spiritually dead. As I said earlier, in our lost condition we are very much half-dead. Ephesians 2:1 describes our condition as "dead in trespasses and sins." At the fall of mankind, humanity fell victim to the thief (John 10:10) who desires nothing more than to steal, kill, and destroy our souls. He didn't rob us of our material possessions but of our relationship with our Creator. Our situation looked hopeless with no chance of restoring our broken relationship with God. Religion couldn't bring us back to life. No amount of good works could resuscitate us. Then, from the most unlikely of sources, our good Samaritan came along. God has done for us what we could not do for ourselves. Look what God did through our good Samaritan, Jesus Christ: "When we were dead in sins, [God] hath quickened us together with Christ, (by grace ye are saved;) and hath raised us up together, and made us sit together in heavenly places in Christ Jesus: that in the ages to come he might show the exceeding riches of his grace in his kindness toward us through Christ Jesus" (Ephesians 2:5–7).

The King of Glory saw our need from heaven and had compassion toward us. He certainly didn't have to make any effort to help us, but His compassion compelled Him to show kindness, love, mercy, and grace toward those who were His enemies. He could have ignored our condition, turned the other way, and pretended not to notice the wounds only He could heal. He could have looked down from heaven, shed a tear, and hoped it would all work out for us. But He chose to come near to us to bind our wounds, and in a display of great personal sacrifice, He made a way for us to be healed. He made a way for us to be brought back to life. He paid a debt He didn't owe without giving any thought to personal benefit. He is our great and mighty Savior. Jesus is the one who provides the example of what it means to love your neighbor.

The world and other people may have used and abused you, chewed you up, and spit you out, but I want you to know God loves you. God is there for you and has drawn near to you. God wants to save you through His Son, Jesus. Whether your wounds are spiritual, emotional, or physical, God desires to see them healed. In turn, God has the expectation that we will show the same type of love, compassion, sacrifice, and selflessness to others in need. "Be kindly affectioned one to another with brotherly love; in honour preferring one another" (Romans 12:10).

I wish I could go back and redo that moment in NYC when I passed by the half-dead man in need. I wish I had acted less like the priest and the Levite and more like the Samaritan—more like Jesus. Obviously, I can't undo what happened, but I can use it as a growth opportunity. It taught me there are half-dead people in need all around. The opportunities to love my neighbor are abundant. The question is, Will I respond to them like the priest and Levite—unconcerned, selfish, distracted, judgmental, sympathetic, but unwilling to sacrifice—or will I be spurred to action by compassion like the Samaritan man? Will I move toward them, do what I can to help, make personal sacrifices, and pay a price I don't owe so they can be healed? Jesus did it for me, and it's the least I can do for someone else. What a different view the world would have of believers in Jesus if we spent less time bickering with one another and more time fighting over who was going to help the half-dead man. Don't pass them by. Don't rationalize your inaction with thoughts of being unqualified or insufficient. God has placed those half-dead people in your path for a reason. Show them the love of Jesus, and lead them to the place of healing—a place where they're fully alive in Christ.

## YOUR LIFE PARABLE

1) Do you find yourself still in the spiritually half-dead state described in this chapter? Have you ever experienced life-giving belief in Jesus Christ? If not, it is time for you to resolve this issue once and for all. I encourage you to follow these three simple steps in prayer to God.
   a. Admit you're a sinner (Romans 3:23).
   b. Believe in the death, burial, and resurrection of Jesus Christ (Romans 10:9–10).
   c. Call on the name of the Lord, asking Him to save you from the penalty of your sin (Romans 10:13).

2) Who did you relate most to in the story of the good Samaritan? The thieves? The priest? The Levite? The Samaritan? What steps do you need to take in your life in order to cultivate a more compassionate heart toward those in need?

3) Who are the half-dead people in your life that you've been ignoring? Pray for them. Take time to go to them and show them the sacrificial love of Jesus.

# 2

## The Storms of Life

***Experiencing peace in the midst of life's most trying times.***

I could tell something was horribly wrong the moment my wife walked through the door. The look of panic on her face was unmistakable. How could something terrible happen at a routine eye exam? During my dozens of visits to the eye doctor, the worst thing I've had happen is their shooting a puff of air into my eye, and the worst news I ever received was that my prescription had worsened over the past year. Maybe it wasn't the eye exam; maybe she'd had an accident or received a bad phone call on her way home from the doctor. Contributing to my concern was the fact that she didn't come right out with what was troubling her. She sat and made small talk until the kids left the room. My son and daughter had barely exited the room when tears began to fill my wife's eyes. I moved closer to her, taking a seat beside her side on the couch. Through her tears and occasional sobs, I learned that she hadn't been in an accident or received bad news in a phone call. The source of her present life storm was, in fact, what she learned at her first-ever routine eye exam to see about getting reading glasses.

Our optometrist happens to be a family friend and neighbor whose kids attended the same school as our two children. The first part of Kerrie's exam was filled with chitchat about kids, work, and life in the neighborhood. After giving the dilating drops a few minutes to work their magic, the doctor used his instruments to peer behind Kerrie's eye at her optic nerve. What he saw caused his countenance and tone to move from casual and friendly to serious and businesslike. His change in demeanor made it obvious to Kerrie that something very serious was wrong. What he saw that caused him such alarm were two extremely swollen optic nerves. At the time this meant absolutely nothing to me. The doctor told her she needed to immediately schedule an appointment with a neuro-ophthalmologist at the University of Pennsylvania Hospital in Philadelphia. He also cautioned her to stay off the internet and not give in to the temptation to google "swollen optic nerves." Of course, what did we do? We googled it and then really started to freak out! We were overwhelmed with the amount of information we found on the web, most of which was extremely scary and negative. The sites we looked at listed a multitude of things that could cause swollen optic nerves, but the scariest two causes were a brain tumor and multiple sclerosis. Why didn't we listen to the doctor and not look on the internet? All the search had done was cause us to worry more and to shed more tears. We were being tossed about in a sea of fear and worry at the mercy of circumstances that were beyond our control. We were in a life storm and experiencing some rough sailing.

Problems (storms) are a part of everyday life. Just like a sailor caught on the stormy and raging sea, we're often tossed to and fro with the winds and waves of life. We feel the wet driving rain rushing down our cheeks in the form of tears. We feel sick to our stomachs as waves of nausea continually lift and drop us. Fear and worry grip us as we wonder if we will make it out of this alive. Life storms come in all shapes and sizes. Sometimes they're brought about by a situation at work—you're fired, caught in the latest downsizing, get demoted, or asked to transfer across the country. Sometimes storms come in our finances—the medical bills pile up, the credit card debt becomes unmanageable, or you're upside down in your house and the creditors are calling. Sometimes the storms are relational—your marriage is falling apart, your kids are rebelling, or your friends have forsaken you in a time of need. Sometimes the storms are physical—there's a lump in your breast, the MRI shows a spot on your lung, or you have a heart attack. Sometimes the storm is ministerial—your church is falling apart, your family disowns you because of your faith, or a longtime friend tragically falls into sin. Sometimes you encounter a Category Five life storm when you're getting hit from every possible angle and you don't feel there is any possible way you're going to survive.

During life storms what one word would you use to describe your situation? *Dire. Anxious. Worried. Troubled. Fearful. Depressed. Overwhelmed. Discouraged. Broken.* What about *peaceful*? Would you use the word *peace* or *peaceful* to describe your situation when you are in the middle of a life storm? No way. Typically peace is the polar opposite of what you experience during the storms of life.

Is peace a genuine possibility during life storms, or is it just a pipedream that we Christians use to attract would-be converts? Is it just a cleverly crafted and effective marketing campaign? "Having a hard time in life right now? Join our team and you too can experience peace!" Is it a bait-and-switch sales technique filled with empty promises? Was Jesus feeding us a line when He said, "Peace I leave with you, my peace I give unto you" (John 14:27)? You really can't blame a person for being somewhat skeptical. We turn on the evening news, and the world seems to be anything but peaceful—there's the war in Iraq, the war on terror, the war on crime, the war on drugs. Peace? I don't think so. Sadly, many believers don't even find God's peace filling their own homes or within their own hearts. We argue with our spouses. We argue with our kids. We fight with our neighbors. We even kick our dogs on occasion. Peace? Not by a long shot.

During my nearly twenty-seven years as a Christian and twenty years as a pastor, I had always toed the party line when it came to peace. I understood and believed the theological implications of the peace with God we have through Christ. It's not that I didn't believe Jesus could give peace, but until recently I had never truly experienced God's unbelievable peace—a peace that passes human comprehension. I'm talking about the practical, day to day peace we all long for in life. But now I know from my own experience that the peace of God is possible even during the most turbulent times of life.

## *LIFE'S STORMY SEAS*

As I struggled through the torrential onslaught of our current life storm and wrestled with God's promise of peace, God led me to a familiar story in Mark 4:35–41. In this passage Jesus and His disciples are caught in a storm so bad that it literally causes the disciples to fear for their lives. I had read this story dozens (if not hundreds) of times, but this time the passage came alive for me, and the truths it contained leapt from the page. I could relate to the disciples' circumstances—wind, waves, rain, and fear. Here they are in the middle of this storm, afraid for their lives, and where's Jesus? Sleeping in the back of the boat! They're being engulfed by this storm, and Jesus is taking a nap. Are you kidding me? The disciples promptly awaken Him and ask Him a very astute question, "Don't You care that we're about to go under?" Or "Hey, Jesus, um, we know You're really tired and all, but do You think You could spare a moment because we're about to die here!"

Have you ever experienced these types of feelings before? You're going through an unbelievable trial, getting knocked about from every possible direction, and it feels like God is asleep. "Hello? Are You up there? Do You see what I'm going through? Do You even care that I'm about to die?" That's how Kerrie and I felt. Here we were in the middle of a Category Five life storm, and when we looked around for help, it seemed that God was sleeping. Didn't He care about our situation? Was He aware of how dire things appeared? If God was awake and on the job, how could He possibly allow something like this to happen? After all, we'd given our lives to Him and were following Him to the best of our ability. We're His children, and you would expect that, as a good parent, He would watch out for our welfare.

After being awakened from His nap, Jesus does something utterly amazing: "And he arose, and rebuked the wind, and said unto the sea, Peace, be still. And the wind ceased, and there was a great calm" (Mark 4:39). At the height of the turbulent storm, Jesus brings peace. He brings a "great calm"— not a normal calm, not an average calm, but a *great* calm. This is a peace and calm unlike any these seasoned fishermen had ever experienced. As a result of this miracle, the disciples begin to ask themselves, "What manner of man is this?" In other words, "Who is this guy?" To say the least, they had a newfound appreciation and reverence for Jesus. This is especially interesting because they had been with Jesus for some time now. They had witnessed Him doing miraculous things in the past, but this was different. They were forever changed as a result. Their fear of the storm and of death was replaced with awe and reverence for Jesus.

As Kerrie and I tossed and tacked through our personal storm, fearful of the outcome, it was as though Jesus stood up in our boat and said, "Peace, be still." We felt a great calm come over us and found our fear and worry replaced with an awe of God like never before. We had both known and walked with Jesus for decades, but this was something new. We were experiencing what Philippians 4:7 describes as "the peace of God." This was a peace the world cannot comprehend—the peace that keeps us anchored when our world is being engulfed. As I basked in this newfound peace, I came to realize that the enduring peace of God is directly linked to three specific areas of peace in my life.

### *PEACE WITH GOD*

At the conclusion of every major conflict in human history, there has usually been some type of peace treaty. Leaders from both sides agree to the terms of surrender and then sign on behalf of their nations as an indication that they intend to live within the agreed-upon provisions. There is no peace without one party surrendering and signing a peace treaty. When an individual accepts Jesus as Savior, he or she has surrendered, and in essence, signed a peace treaty with God. It is a peace treaty signed with the blood of Jesus Christ (Romans 5:1; Colossians 1:20–21). Why is this important? Because it's not possible to have the genuine "peace of God" without first having "peace with God." Experiencing the peace of God that passes understanding flows from understanding that Jesus shed His blood so you could have eternal peace with

God. To experience God's unbelievable peace, our personal peace with God must move beyond a one-time decision to be born again. As we navigate through life, we must learn to continually rest in our peaceful relationship with God. It should not only impact our hereafter but should drastically change our here and now. Through Jesus we have become children of God. As our heavenly Father, God always has our best interest at heart. Though we may not always understand it, God is lovingly orchestrating the affairs of our lives.

Looking back to the beginning of Mark's account of the storm, we see that Jesus sets out a very clear plan for the disciples. "And the same day, when the even was come, he saith unto them, Let us pass over unto the other side. And when they had sent away the multitude, they took him even as he was in the ship" (Mark 4:35–36). Who says they should sail to the other side of the sea? Who leads them directly into the storm? Jesus does. I know Jesus is no Al Roker, meteorologist extraordinaire, but as the Creator of the universe He knows what awaits them. Jesus is no doubt fully aware that during their journey across the sea they will encounter one of the scariest storms they've ever experienced. In spite of this knowledge, Jesus allows them, even commands them, to set out on a course that will be stormy.

Is there any doubt that Jesus loves His disciples? I think that's irrefutable. He loves them so much He's willing to die for them on the cross. He will bear the wrath of God so they (and we) can be reconciled to God. It's safe to say He cares for them and wants what's best for them. Looking through the storm and to the conclusion, we begin to understand Jesus' reason for allowing His followers to experience the storm. Without the storm they could not have truly experienced the peace and great calm. Jesus becomes more real to them as a result of seeing Him work in the midst of the storm. Their fear of the storm and of death is replaced with a healthy fear of God. The disciples grow in their awe of Jesus as a result of going through the storm. They ask, "What manner of man is this?" They now realize if He can control the wind and the sea, He can handle whatever life might throw at them. They experience God's unbelievable peace because they're resting in their relationship with Him, knowing that He's looking out for them.

As I mentioned earlier, there are times when it feels like Jesus is asleep in the boat while we endure the onslaught of life's latest storm. What I've come to realize is that God's apparent lack of interest is really a lovingly orchestrated opportunity for me to grow in my love for Him and to experience the peace of God. He's not asleep on the job, He's dreaming up new ways to manifest Himself to me. God's love for the world is immense and boundless. His love is evidenced by the fact that He sacrificed His beloved Son for us. It, therefore, doesn't stand to reason that He would carelessly forsake us in our greatest time of need. To the contrary, as a loving Father, He's working in our lives to bring us to a deeper love for Him. He desires to see us grow in our faith and awe of Him. That said, we must realize that what's best for us isn't always what is easiest for us. Struggle, and sometimes pain, is often the price of growth. Sometimes God has to put us flat on our backs so that we have nowhere to look but up. From our limited, earthly perspective, we're primarily concerned with our personal comfort. From God's infinite, eternal perspective He's primarily concerned with our personal growth. As a result of the storm, the disciples grew in their relationship with Jesus. As a result of our life storms we have an opportunity for growth. We have peace with God through the blood of Jesus Christ, but we must learn to rest in that fact, realizing that the events of our life, rough as they may be, drive us toward Him.

### *PEACE WITHIN MYSELF*

Andrew, James, and John rowed with all their might as Peter barked out commands that got lost in the howl of wind ripping through the sails. Their arms and backs ached as they rowed against the enormous waves crashing against their small vessel. Their calloused hands were on fire as new blisters grew with each synchronized pull of the oars. Wind and rain whipped horizontally across the boat and strung their faces like a thousand small bees. The rest of the disciples did their best to bail water over the side, but the battle was futile. For every bucket of water they bailed, two more spilled over the side as another wave smashed into the side of the boat. Matthew loses his lunch over the side of boat and is reminded why he hates the sea, sailing, and seafood. Their effort is valiant but in vain. All their experience, all their strength, all their pride is no match for this storm. They can't believe that after so many years of working on the sea without so much as a scratch, they are going to die during a routine sail from one side of the lake to the other. Exhausted, soaked, sick, and filled with fear these seasoned fishermen and experienced sailors finally relinquish control and turn to the one who governs the elements.

In the middle of our life storm, we worked hard to come up with a plan that would make everything better. We rowed until our hands bled. We bailed water as fast as we could in hopes of saving the ship. Our stomachs turned with every crashing wave. I found myself frequently muttering six simple words, "What am I going to do?" Sandwiched in the middle of this sentence was my main problem. "I" was trying to control this situation. After all "I" had been working at this Christian thing for nearly thirty years, not to mention I had spent well over half that in "full-time ministry." Certainly, "I" knew what "I" was doing. In reality I was like the little Dutch boy trying to put his fingers in the holes of the leaky dam. It wasn't long before I was out of digits, and the water was rising over my head.

This is a common occurrence in the lives of believers. We battle God for control. We get locked into intense power struggles with God Almighty. It sounds incredibly silly, but for some strange reason we think we can handle life's toughest situations better than He can. When we try to control our situation rather than acknowledging that He is in control, we are robbed of peace. Paul says it this way, "And *let* the peace of God *rule* in your hearts" (Colossians 3:15, emphasis added).

First, we must let God's peace rule within us. We must allow it to reside in our hearts. It's interesting that many times we try to blame the lack of peace in our lives on our circumstances or on God's lack of interest in us when in reality the problem lies within us. In many ways our stormy lives are a reflection of our stormy hearts. We haven't allowed the peace to inhabit us because we're trying to control the situation ourselves. God won't impose His peace on us. He doesn't require us to live a life of peace. Peace is available; it is at our disposal, but in order to have it, we have to let Him in. The disciples had to come to Jesus and ask Him to get involved in their situation. Once they opened the door of His involvement, the peace came flooding in. Don't miss how hard it must have been for the disciples to ask for Jesus' help. After all, they were experienced fishermen and knowledgeable sailors, and He was a carpenter. They had to admit they were incapable of handling the situation at hand and let Jesus get involved. This is a huge admission, and it made all the difference in the world. I'm reminded of the popular Christian saying, "Let go and let God!" When we loosen our grip and turn things over to God, something miraculous happens. It's in these moments of apparent weakness that God shows Himself strong on our behalf (2 Corinthians 12:9).

Second, we must let God's peace "rule" within us. God has established His kingdom in our hearts, but are we allowing Him to rule? Who, or what, is sitting on the throne of your heart? If the throne of your heart is occupied by anything, or anyone, other than Jesus, then peace will always elude you. It can even be good things that are stealing God's rightful place in your life. As the battle for control rages within our members, we will never experience the peace of God. How do you determine who, or what, is on your heart's throne? In a word, *love*. Whatever you love is on the throne of your heart. If God is your number-one love, then He is ruling over your life. This fact will be supported by how you live and how you handle life storms. It's one thing to say God is number one in your life and quite another to actually live like it.

There are some very obvious areas of your life you can look at to determine whether or not God is on your heart's throne. First, how do you spend your *time*? Take a look at your calendar, and see if time with God or time serving God is a priority in your life. Second, how do you spend your *treasure*? Flip through your credit card statement, and see where the majority of your spending is being directed— that's your number-one love. Third, what do you *talk* about? Out of the abundance of the heart the mouth speaks (Luke 6:45). If you love God and He's ruling in your life, you can't help but talk about Him.

Once Kerrie and I relinquished control of our situation, God's peace flooded our hearts. We held up the white flag and surrendered to His rule. The choice to let God's peace rule within us is a day-by-day, moment-by-moment decision. We have to constantly be asking ourselves, "Who's in control?" or "Who's calling the shots right now?" Never forget— peace requires surrender. Without complete and unconditional surrender, there is no lasting peace. The lordship of Jesus in life requires obedience and submission. I'm placing myself beneath Him. I'm His vessel, and He can use me and do with me as He chooses. I will do what He asks of me even when I don't understand all the particulars of the situation.

In Mark's account of the storm I find that question asked by the disciples to be incredibly insightful. "What manner of man is this, that even the wind and the sea obey him?" (Mark 4:41). Did you catch that? The wind and the sea *obey* Him. Why don't we? All the elements of the creation operate in submission to His commands, and yet humans struggle to give Him free rein in their lives. Give up the fight, wave your white flag, and unconditionally surrender control of your life to Jesus. Place yourself in submission to His lordship. What do you receive in return? Peace that passes understanding.

### *PEACE WITH OTHERS*

Without question, the most tortuous portion of any life storm involves relational unrest with people close to us. The knowledge that someone is displeased with us causes us to slide into a place of despair. Relational conflict and turmoil often rob us of God's peace. When our relationships stink—life stinks! As the disciples faced their real life storm, they had a relational problem with Jesus Himself. His apparent lack of concern was the cause of serious friction between Him and the disciples: "Don't You care that we are about to die?"

Throughout life we face a multitude of relational storms that have peace-stealing potential. Anytime you have two people in close proximity to one another for an extended period of time, there will eventually be conflict. How do we keep relational conflict from robbing us of God's peace? I think a passage in Romans 12 provides the best solution to this dilemma, "If it be possible, as much as lieth in you, live peaceably with all men" (Romans 12:18). The truth contained in this verse is simple but also quite liberating. It assures us that our main responsibility in relational conflict is to do the best we can to maintain peace. We can't make people be at peace with us, but we can make our very best effort ("as much as lieth in you") to live harmoniously with them. The results are up to them and God. We can do everything right, and people may still have a problem with us. If we're resting in the fact that we have done all that we can do and have followed God's Word, we can have the peace of God despite another person's refusal to live harmoniously.

The ability to live this out is a matter of where we seek our approval. Most people feel a strong need to be approved of by others. Some people find their sense of worth in how others view them: "If people like me, then my worth is increased, but if people don't like me, then I'm worth less." Even the most independent sorts struggle with the need to be liked or approved of by others. I know this because I'm one of those independent sorts. No rational person likes to think that someone is displeased with him. Gaining victory over this and rediscovering God's peace result from seeking the approval of God rather than the approval of man.

A great deal of our life is spent trying to figure out what pleases those people closest to us so that we can give them what they desire and avoid those things that cause them to be displeased with us. This is true of our spouses, our kids, our bosses, our congregants, and even our pets. Over time we compile an extensive list of what things please the people in our circle of influence, and then wear ourselves out trying to keep everyone happy. We have to change our focus and become more concerned about what pleases God than what pleases everyone else. If we genuinely feel our actions are pleasing to God, then people's disapproval will not steal our peace. We'll never please everyone, so the best option is to make sure we're pleasing God first and foremost. This is not to say that we live in blatant disregard for what pleases people, especially those who are closest to us, and then blame it on God. According to Jesus, the second most important commandment is to love your neighbor as yourself. You need to be concerned for others and their needs. However, the fulfilling of the second commandment must flow from the first commandment, which is to love God with the entirety of your being. Make loving God and pleasing God your number-one priority, and your peace will not vanish at the first sign of relational turmoil. It comes down to this simple question, "Who are you living for?"

### *PEACE, BE STILL*

Kerrie and I made the hour-long trek to her first doctor's appointment at the University of Pennsylvania Medical Center filled with God's peace. We met with her neuro-ophthalmologist and discussed her situation and course of action. The days that followed were filled with numerous tests as Kerrie was repeatedly poked, prodded, and scanned. We continued to pray and ask God for His unbelievable peace in this storm. Prepared for the worst, but expecting the best, we once again traveled to Philadelphia to meet with Kerrie's doctor to review the results of all her tests. As we entered the hospital that day, I could still feel the sting of the driving rain against my face as the storm raged. I still felt twinges of doubt wondering if the boat was going to sink beneath the swells of our Category Five storm. However, overriding all of that was *peace*—a stillness and great calm that can't be explained in human terms.

Kerrie and I sat in the doctor's office holding hands as the doctor delivered his diagnosis— *pseudo-tumor*. What? What's that? I knew *tumor* was not good, but the *pseudo* part threw me. I knew *pseudo* meant fake or false, but I had never heard that term attached to the word *tumor*. The doctor went on to explain that Kerrie didn't have a mass in her brain, but her optic nerve was swollen and showing signs of a tumor. Her symptoms indicated a tumor, but there was none (i.e., pseudo-tumor). This was a serious condition but could be treated with medication and a change in diet. Given the multiplicity of things it could have been, this was great news! It really couldn't have turned out any better, and we praise God for the outcome. But what if it hadn't been good news? What if it had been MS or a malignant brain tumor? Please hear me when I tell you with one hundred percent certainty that peace would have prevailed. Would we have been upset? No question. Peace doesn't mean freedom from emotion. Even if things hadn't been OK, we would have been OK with it.

We rest in our peace with God and realize He loves us and is with us no matter the circumstances or outcome. Even in times of apparent unconcern, He's orchestrating every raindrop and has our best interest at heart. Our peace flows deep within us as a result of surrendering control of our lives and all of life's circumstances to the Lord. We find peace in knowing that we're doing all we can to live in a manner that's pleasing to Him. Anyone can have peace when things are going great, but God's unbelievable peace is found in the middle of life's perfect storm. The one that rebuked the wind and the rain can cause a great calm and stillness to enter into our hearts. The storm may rage on, but we can rest knowing we're anchored to the giver of the peace that passes all understanding.

## YOUR LIFE PARABLE

1) What life storm are you experiencing right now? Get honest with God and pour out your heart to Him about the emotions you're experiencing in this storm. Ask Him to give you strength to trust Him through the storm.

2) How has a past or present life storm caused you to draw closer to God?

3) Peace requires surrender. In what ways are you battling God for control as you attempt to navigate your life storm?

# 3

## The Gifted Life

***Watching God take our limited resources and use them in limitless ways.***

Dozens of small brown faces looked up at me, their eyes squinting against the tropical sun. At six-foot-six, I was a giant to most of them, and they were in awe of the basketball player from America who had come halfway around the world to instruct them. I looked back at them with equal amazement. However, my amazement was not directed at them but at God. How did He do this? I was in southern India about to conduct a basketball clinic while at the same time hopefully being a witness for my Lord and Savior. Who was I to be given such a tremendous opportunity? The truthful answer is that, from a worldly perspective, I was a nobody. I was an unknown small-college basketball player from the Midwest, and yet God was about to use my meager gifts in a huge way. I was about to instruct a group of kids about basketball and Jesus Christ on the other side of the world. How does a person come to the point in their Christian walk where he is used mightily in the advancement of God's kingdom? How do we experience God using us in a way that far exceeds our wildest expectations? For me, it was tied to a simple decision made decades earlier as a college student. Before we get into my decision, I want to look at a decision made by another young man that resulted in him being used by God in a miraculous way.

## *A LITTLE BOY'S LUNCH*

The sun fills the blue sky with all its splendor; there's not so much as a hint of a cloud in the sky. The scent of jasmine fills the air as the birds lift up a beautiful melody of praise to their Creator. It's a glorious spring morning in the city of Bethsaida—in a word, perfection! A young boy sits in a chair, stooped over, near the front door of his humble abode. He hurriedly tries to fasten his sandals so he can get out the door. He's supposed to meet his friends down by the lake for a day filled with adventures—rock climbing, cliff-diving, and spear-fishing to name a few. He finishes latching his sandals, grabs his gear, and takes a step toward the front door as his mom calls out from the back room of the house, "Did you pack your lunch?" His response is typical of any kid in any culture, "Oh, Mom! I'm going to be late! I'm not even hungry!" Her response is also classic, "Don't you set foot out of this house until I've packed you a lunch."

Years of trying have taught him that arguing with her is futile. Rather than further delay his departure, he quickly relents and waits for her to pack his lunch. Sensing his restlessness, his mother hastily packs his lunch, hands him the bag, and gives him a kiss on the top of the head. The boy turns on his heels and bolts for the front door, shouting the mandatory "Love you" to his mother as the door slams behind him. Upon leaving the house, he glances into the bag to see what his mom has packed for his lunch—five small loaves of bread and two small fish. His immediate thought is, "Oh man, the fellas are gonna make fun of me for this!" He contemplates tossing the bag lunch in the trash as he rounds the corner to head out of town, but he stops himself after considering the possibility of working out a lunch trade with one of his friends. "John likes fish. Maybe he'll be up for a swap."

Lunch in hand, he dashes down the street and makes his way toward the Sea of Galilee. He's almost to their normal rendezvous spot when he notices a huge crowd of people gathering around. He's never seen such a large group of people. There must be ten or fifteen thousand people. "What could they possibly be doing? What in the world is going on?" Whatever it is, he doesn't want to miss it. His friends can wait a few minutes; he's got to check out what is going on. He methodically squeezes his way through the crowd and makes his way toward what appears to be the center of attention. As the sea of people parts, he finally catches a glimpse of who is causing such a large gathering. When he first sees the man, he's a little confused because he can't understand why all these people are gathering around this ordinary looking rabbi. It doesn't take long before he realizes why this group has gathered. This ordinary looking man is performing extraordinary feats—the lame walk, the blind see, the dumb speak. Not only is He performing miraculous feats, but the words that He speaks are profound and rock the young man to his very core. He's never heard anyone speak like this before. The rabbis at the synagogue are so dull and boring, but this guy speaks with authority and great sensitivity. The young man is so captivated that he has soon forgotten about meeting his buddies. He spends the entire day walking with the crowd, watching the man perform miracles, and listening to Him speak about the things of God and His kingdom. The more he sees and the more he listens, the more mesmerized he becomes with this man of God. He now understands why such a large crowd has gathered and is following him around the countryside.

The boy's stomach suddenly lets out an embarrassingly loud growl that reminds him, and everyone else, that he hasn't eaten all day. After several more intense tummy rumbles, the boy suddenly remembers, "My lunch!" He quickly finds a spot still within earshot of the Miracle Worker, sits down, and prepares to dig into his lunch of fish and bread. Just as he's about to sink his teeth into the first bite, he overhears the man and his followers having a discussion. The man's followers seem frustrated and perplexed, but the man remains unflappable. His eyes glint with a confidence that He knows something that no one else does. The boy rises from his spot and inches closer so he can hear what they're saying. They're talking about food. The whole crowd is hungry, but they don't have enough food or money to feed this massive crowd. The boy glances down at his bag of bread and fish and then slowly turns his eyes toward the Miracle Worker. "What should I do?" he thinks. Suddenly his stomach lets out another monstrous howl, which almost sounds like, "Feed me!" His eyes once more fall on the lunch his mom packed for him, but then he looks back at the Wonder Worker. He knows what he must do. He hurries over to one of the disciples standing on the edge of the crowd and gently tugs on his garment. The disciple turns to find the young boy beaming at him with a smile from ear to ear, lunch bag extended. After eyeing the contents of the bag, the disciple is tempted to send the boy away, but he remembers how upset his master got the last time they shooed away a group of kids. As ridiculous as it appears, he thinks the safe play would be to bring this kid to the Master and let Him decide what to do with his bag lunch. What happens next is absolutely amazing.

### *THE TESTING OF PHILIP*

"When Jesus then lifted up his eyes, and saw a great company come unto him, he saith unto Philip, Whence shall we buy bread, that these may eat? And this he said to prove him: for he himself knew what he would do. Philip answered him, Two hundred pennyworth of bread is not sufficient for them, that every one of them may take a little" (John 6:5–7).

Jesus turns his attention to Philip, who was from the nearby town of Bethsaida. He's not picking on Philip but wants to see where he is spiritually. He's asking him this question to prove him. Philip's response shows that his perspective is limited to his natural eyes and the ability of man. He says it would take approximately six months' worth of salary for them to be able to give everyone a snack. The need is too great for any provision they can deliver. His response is not dissimilar to ours when God places us in situations that look impossible from our perspective. When we look through natural eyes, the problem seems insurmountable, and any solutions we concoct appear to be drastically insufficient. It's in those "throw your hands up in the air" moments that we must realize God is testing our faith. He wants us to turn our eyes away from the circumstances and onto Christ, away from our situation and toward our Savior. To us, it seems impossible, and we have no idea what we're going to do. But Jesus knew what He was going to do before he asked Philip the question. He knows His capabilities in your situation as well.

When our problem seems big, it's because our God has become small. When our view of God is big, it will make the problems of life seem small. When this happens in our lives, we're looking at things from the proper perspective—from God's perspective. In hindsight, Philip's answer should have been something along the lines of, "I don't know what we're going to do, but You're Lord of all, and I'm sure You'll figure something out." That's always a fair response to God when we face life's impossible situations: "I don't know what to do about this, Lord, but I know You have a solution." About the time Jesus and Philip are finishing up their little talk, Andrew shows up with our hero in tow.

### *THE DOUBTING OF ANDREW*

"One of his disciples, Andrew, Simon Peter's brother, saith unto him, There is a lad here, which hath five barley loaves, and two small fishes: but what are they among so many?" (John 6:8–9). Andrew comes strolling into the conversation between Jesus and Philip, opens the boy's bag lunch, and announces the contents to the group—five barley loaves and a couple of fish. I love the dichotomy that exists within Andrew. On the one hand, he brings the boy and his lunch to Jesus because he thinks this may be a possible solution to their problem. After all, he has seen his Master do some unbelievable things over the last couple of years. Maybe this could be another chance for Jesus to show the people of Israel that He's the Messiah. On the other hand, when he steps into the circle of his peers, he suddenly realizes how foolish it seems to think that a few loaves of bread and a couple of pieces of fish could feed a crowd of five thousand plus. As a result, he proposes the idea to Jesus and the group but immediately offers a qualifier: "But what are they among so many?" He doesn't want to look stupid, so he squashes his own idea.

Like Philip (and us), Andrew has fallen into the trap of looking at circumstances through natural eyes rather than supernatural eyes. Andrew did what he could naturally do—he brought the lunch to Jesus. Now he needed to allow Jesus to do the "super" part. What the boy offered seemed insignificant, but in the hands of Jesus, nothing is inconsequential.

As followers of Jesus we know He is capable of supernatural things. The Bible leaves no doubt about His power. The book of Colossians describes Jesus this way, "For by him were all things created, that are in heaven, and that are in earth, visible and invisible, whether they be thrones, or dominions, or principalities, or powers: all things were created by him, and for him: and he is before all things, and by him all things consist" (Colossians 1:16–17). He created everything, and by Him all things are held together. I think He can handle our problem. We know this intellectually. We may have even seen Him do some miraculous things in our own lives or in the lives of others. However, there's still a seed of doubt that creeps into our minds as the natural man begins to contemplate how foolish we look when we come to Jesus with the equivalent of a fish sandwich and ask Him to feed a hungry mob. We must resist the tendency to lower our focus to the realm of the natural and instead keep our eyes firmly fixed on the Miracle Worker. In His hands the insignificant becomes substantial, and the minuscule become enormous.

## *PARTAKING IN A MIRACLE*

"And Jesus said, Make the men sit down. Now there was much grass in the place. So the men sat down, in number about five thousand. And Jesus took the loaves; and when he had given thanks, he distributed to the disciples, and the disciples to them that were set down; and likewise of the fishes as much as they would. When they were filled, he said unto his disciples, Gather up the fragments that remain, that nothing be lost. Therefore they gathered them together, and filled twelve baskets with the fragments of the five barley loaves, which remained over and above unto them that had eaten" (John 6:10–13). What happens next is undoubtedly one of Jesus' most famous and mind-blowing miracles.

From the beginning of this dilemma, Jesus never expects the disciples or the little boy to solve this monumental problem. He's not asking them to give something or do something beyond their capability—like Philip's suggestion of spending six months' worth of salary so everyone can have a snack. They don't have that kind of money, and besides, it wouldn't adequately solve the issue anyway. All Jesus wants is for them to give what they have and allow Him to work. If only all those involved will place themselves and what they have in His very capable hands, He can take it and use it for His glory. We often fall into the trap of basing our involvement on our ability to solve the entire problem. If we don't have the necessary resources, skills, or tools, we throw up our hands and do nothing. All Jesus wants from us is to give Him what we have, and He'll take care of the rest.

I love the progression that is laid out in the verses that follow. First, Jesus takes what has been given by the little boy, and then He gives thanks, blesses it, and multiplies it. Second, Jesus gives the multiplied bread and fish to the disciples. Finally, He asks the disciples to take what they have been given and distribute it to those who are hungry. Notice how Jesus involves His followers in the performance of this miracle. God uses human instruments to carry out His work. Jesus takes what we bring to Him and He blesses it and multiplies it. He is the Miracle Worker. He is the one who puts the "super" in supernatural. We give and He then gives back to us in abundance. But this doesn't complete the process. We are not the end, but rather a means to an end. We are then to take the blessing that we've been given and bless others with it so that their needs can be met. You have been blessed so that you can be a blessing to others.

With Philip's solution, everyone in the crowd would have received a few bites, but when Jesus gets involved, everyone gets to eat their fill. If they had kept on eating, Jesus would have kept on multiplying. In fact, the passage says that Jesus made so much that they had twelve baskets of leftovers. God always gives us more than we really need. Jesus asks the disciples to gather up the fragments, and there's one basket per disciple. Could these twelve baskets of leftovers be an object lesson for the disciples? As they carry those large baskets full of leftover bread and fish, they are no doubt reminded that this abundance came from five barley loaves and two fish. They have to be in awe of the fact that Jesus has fed so many with so little. Here's the point I don't want you to miss: God can take your limited resources and use them in limitless ways. Don't allow your view of the contribution you can make to keep you from giving generously. God blesses our generosity and uses it to perform miracles in the lives of those in need.

"Then those men, when they had seen the miracle that Jesus did, said, This is of a truth that prophet that should come into the world" (John 6:14). Jesus' fame increased as a result of what happened. People didn't walk away from this event talking about the generosity of the little boy who gave his lunch. They didn't leave marveling at the efficiency with which the disciples distributed the bread and fish. When they thought about that day they thought about one person—Jesus. He was the Miracle Worker. He was the one responsible for filling their need. It was Jesus who got the credit for what happened. This may seem like a rather obvious and meaningless issue to raise, but it's a central concept that we absolutely must understand. All we do in life, all we give, all the help we offer is for Jesus' honor and glory. It's not about us; it's about Him. Christianity has too many celebrities when it should have only one! We never find out the name of the boy who offered his lunch to Jesus, but we do know the name of the one who used it to feed five thousand plus people that day. You may never be famous. Your name may never be up in lights. But you can use the resources at your disposal to make the name of Jesus famous. In a world that applauds self-promotion, the followers of Jesus are about selflessly promoting our Savior.

### *MY LUNCH*

"What can I possibly do? Really! What do I have to offer that could possibly make any difference?" These were the thoughts troubling my mind as a twenty-year-old college student with no income, no job, no other skills besides being a decent student and a pretty good athlete. I had no spiritual training. To say my knowledge of the Bible was limited would be being kind. There are so many people who are in need and so many people who need to know Jesus. I wanted to help, but I didn't have the tools to make any difference whatsoever. That's when it hit me, God was not asking me to be or give something I didn't possess. He simply wanted me to be obedient with what I did possess. What did I have? What was in my hand, so to speak? A basketball. A spherical compilation of leather, rubber, and air. *This* was what God wanted me to give? How could God possibly use a big orange ball to bring Himself honor and glory? That was not *my* issue. Mine was not to question "why" or "how" but to answer the call of "what." God wanted me to use my basketball skills to serve Him, and so that's what I did.

As a new believer in Jesus Christ, I was like the little boy with the bag lunch. What I possessed seemed ordinary enough, and I wasn't real sure how it could be of any use to further God's kingdom and minister to the needs I observed all around me. At the time I became a believer, I was on a basketball scholarship at a college in Kansas City, Missouri, and I decided to leverage those skills for the glory of God. God had given me the athletic abilities I possessed, and now I was giving them back to Him and asking Him to use them as He saw fit. What resulted was something I could have never imagined. In the years since I made that simple decision, God has allowed me to coach in children's basketball leagues and to start competitive basketball leagues that included major college and pro players and that involved the sharing of the gospel before each game. He allowed me to share my faith with a number of college teammates, many of whom came to Christ as a result. (Several of them are now in the ministry and serving the Lord faithfully.) In addition to all that is my recent opportunity to conduct a basketball clinic halfway around the world in southern India. I can truly say that God has gone beyond my wildest imaginations when it comes to using a big orange ball for His glory. My view of what I possessed was very much like Philip and Andrew's view of the boy's lunch. I was looking at things from a worldly perspective. I viewed what I had to offer as inconsequential. What could putting an orange ball through a metal hoop possibly do to impact the world? God had a different view. God's concern wasn't with the amount I had to offer but with my obedience in offering what I had been given.

After following Jesus for many years, I've come to realize we all have a "lunch" to offer Jesus. Some have larger lunches than others, but everyone has something to offer. I also now understand that over time, our lunch can take different forms. I'm getting to the age where playing and teaching basketball is a less viable option. However, as one door closes, another opens. No matter your status in life, you have something to offer. You can bring something to Jesus that He can take and multiply for His honor and glory. The question before us is, "What's in your lunch bag? What gifts and abilities do you have to offer Jesus? What monetary or material possessions can you offer to Jesus so that He can perform miracles?"

## *ARE YOU GOING TO EAT THAT?*

As we read this story in Scripture, our tendency is to think the little boy had no other option but to bring his lunch to Jesus. As I see it, the little boy had at least four options for his lunch. They are the same four options we have when it comes to offering our lives to Jesus—the wasted life, the selfish life, the generous life, or the sacrificial life.

## *THE WASTED LIFE*

I am consistently convicted about the amount of food my family wastes. After each meal our garbage can is practically overflowing with uneaten portions of what was served. When my frustration builds to the breaking point, I roll out my standard "Little Kids Are Starving in Africa" speech, which helps for a day or two, but then we fall right back into the same old pattern of wastefulness. As the young boy in our story left his home that morning, he could have thrown his lunch in the garbage where it would have rotted, gone to waste, and been of no use to anyone. Later in the day when he wanted the lunch or saw that it could have been of use to someone else, he would have been filled with regret but unable to reverse his decision to waste his lunch.

While wasting food is certainly awful, there's nothing more tragic than watching someone waste his or her life. To see a life filled with potential and promise end with unfulfilled dreams brings great sadness into my heart. I can't imagine what it does to the heart of God. He's the one who has given us all we possess. He's the only one who knows our full potential. When we waste the gifts and resources He has given to us, we end up with a regret-filled life. A life of regret, consumed by missed opportunities, is a miserable existence. Frankly, too many followers of Jesus live wasted lives. You're a unique creation of God Almighty that's filled with unlimited potential. You have so much to offer. You can have an eternal impact if you simply take advantage of the opportunities God is giving to you to serve Him. Offer back to Him the gifts He has given you. Don't waste your lunch; give it to Jesus and allow Him to help you reach your full potential.

### *THE SELFISH LIFE*

The most obvious option for the hungry boy would have been for him to eat his own lunch. After all, it was his, and he was hungry. His mother had the foresight to pack a lunch for him, and he was entitled to enjoy it. Those without food should have done a better job of preparing, and then they wouldn't have been starving at the end of the day. While the text doesn't give any indication about the validity of my next comment, I am convinced there were other people in this crowd who had food. Think about it, a group of five thousand plus and no one but this little boy thought to bring a sandwich? I suspect there were many people in the crowd that day that had food but chose to act in a selfish way and consume their lunch themselves. They knew there was a need; they knew Jesus and his disciples were looking for food; but they made the conscious decision to look out for themselves first. No one would have blamed the boy for eating the lunch he brought. I'm sure he was famished and his stomach was saying, "Feed me!" However, he made a decision that went against his nature and his flesh. He did something that was contrary to the decision most people would have made under those circumstances.

To live in a selfish manner is incredibly common. It's in our nature to be selfish. What's one of the first words kids learn to say? "*Mine*!" Did you teach your darling child to be a selfish brat who hoards all the toys at the play date? No, it's hardwired into them. Though we grow more adept at covering up our selfish tendencies, the penchant remains within us throughout life. Our selfishness grows beyond toys, and we become very protective of "*my* time, *my* money, *my* stuff, *my* job, *my* ministry, *my* talents." We're perpetual two-year-olds focused on what is "Mine!" Too often we take the things God has given us and consume them for our own benefit. This mentality finds its origins in the attitude that we alone are responsible for our giftedness and accomplishments. We aren't wasting things God has provided, but we certainly aren't using them for the benefit of anyone other than ourselves.

## *THE GENEROUS LIFE*

Let's assume that the young lad in our story is a good kid, a very conscientious young man who is concerned about the welfare of others. When he sits down to eat his lunch, he notices the wearied, hungry faces of the people next to him. He feels bad that he has food and they don't and decides to share his lunch with them. He divides the five loaves and two fish among his small group and is able to give about ten people a little nourishment. They're not stuffed by any stretch, but at least they aren't going to faint because they are so famished. If we observed this happen, we would commend the actions of the young boy, pat him on the head, and tell him what a good thing he did. He did what he could do to help people who were in need. He did a good thing, but was it the *best* thing?

The world is filled with people who are legitimately concerned about the welfare of their fellow human beings, and they do all that is within their power to help. We continually see people rush into tragic situations and help people who are suffering through natural disasters, war, famine, disease, and various crimes against humanity. The problem is that we never seem to make a dent in the problems we're battling. As much as we do, it never seems to be enough. We give what we can, but the enormity of the need overwhelms our generosity. Humanitarian and philanthropic efforts do a lot of good in the world, but their impact is limited because people often fail to involve the Miracle Worker in their efforts. The point is that alone we can make a minor impact, but with Jesus' involvement we can make a massive impact.

### *THE SACRIFICIAL LIFE*

We know what the boy ended up doing—he offered what he had to Jesus. He made a decision to sacrifice what he had and give it to Jesus. This was obviously the right choice, but it wasn't the easiest or most practical decision. He didn't know what Jesus was going to do with his offering—toss it aside and dismiss it as inconsequential, feed it to the birds, share it with the disciples, or even just eat it Himself. What happened was truly miraculous. His meager gift was used to bless thousands of people. Jesus took his gift and did far more than he could have done by himself. Keep in mind that the boy was part of the crowd of people who got to eat their fill that day. He got back much more than he had given. Can you imagine the satisfaction that filled him as he sat at the feet of Jesus partaking of the feast He was miraculously providing? What joy and fulfillment must have filled his soul as he realized that his small gift had resulted in Jesus impacting thousands! With each loaf of bread and piece of fish his sense of contentment must have increased exponentially.

Romans 12:1 describes the sacrificial life God desires His followers to lead: "I beseech you therefore, brethren, by the mercies of God, that ye present your bodies a living sacrifice, holy, acceptable unto God, which is your reasonable service." What does God want from you? Your entire life! What? That seems a bit radical, doesn't it? On the contrary, God views this type of sacrifice as "reasonable." The boy in our story brought everything he had to Jesus—no more, no less. God has the same expectation of us as His followers. He doesn't ask us to bring something we don't possess, but He does ask us to offer what's in our lunch. When we do, miracles happen, and in the process we get blessed. Jesus can take our gift and use it to impact more people than we could possibly affect on our own. God can take our limited resources and use them in limitless ways. With our offering comes a sense of satisfaction, fulfillment, contentment, and joy from knowing we did all that we could do to serve our Master and help our fellow man.

How do we get to the point of living a sacrificial life? How do we turn the corner and begin living more selflessly? I think the process starts by understanding the source of all you are and have. When we realize everything we are and all we possess are gifts from God, it becomes easier to relinquish control and give it back to Him. When our mentality is that we earned what we have and or we worked hard to get where we are, then our willingness to do anything but look out for ourselves will be lessened. The bottom line is this; we are blessed in order to be a blessing. God hasn't given you all that you have (time, talent, and treasure) so that you can waste it, consume it, or even just share it. He gave it to you so you could offer it back to Him and watch as He impacts thousands.

### *WHAT'S IN YOUR LUNCH?*

You are incredibly gifted! You have more to offer than you can possibly imagine. Do some people have more than others? Yes, without question. But with God the issue is never quantity. He is infinitely more interested in willingness and obedience than He is in how much we bring to the table. In Matthew 25, Jesus tells a story of three individuals who received varying amounts of resources over which they were given stewardship. The master in this story expects the three stewards to take what they've been given and turn a profit. On his return the master holds the three stewards accountable for what they have done with what they were given. Two of the three double the amounts they were given and receive the exact same commendation from the master even though they had different amounts to work with at the beginning. The third servant, in essence, wastes his opportunity and is severely chastised by the master. Don't get caught up in how much you have or don't have to offer. Don't fall into the trap of comparing yourself to other people because that only leads to one of two things: pride or feelings of worthlessness. In either case you're rendered ineffective for the King. Know that you have been gifted according to

God's purposes (1 Corinthians 12:18), and focus on offering back to Him whatever gifts He has given you.

The world around us is filled with physical, emotional, and spiritual needs. We have the gifts at our disposal to meet those needs if we will simply surrender control to the Miracle Worker. Each of us has 86,400 seconds to spend each day; how can we best utilize them for Jesus? Each of us has been given a pool of financial resources for which we are responsible; how can we best utilize them for Jesus? Each of us has been given talents and gifts beyond measure; how will we best utilize them for Jesus? All that you are and all that you have can and should be leveraged for the kingdom of God. Don't discount your ability to make an impact because the need looks so great compared to the resources you bring to the table. Be willing, be obedient, and then leave the multiplying part to Jesus. In those moments of life when I begin to doubt the potential impact of my meager lunch, I'm reminded of what Paul wrote regarding the ability of God, "Now unto him that is able to do exceeding abundantly above all that we ask or think, according to the power that worketh in us" (Ephesians 3:20). God's ability exceeds our wildest imagination. He's the one with all the power. Bring your lunch, and let Him go to work.

### *GOD'S STICK*

Let me illustrate this concept with a famous story from the Old Testament. Moses was an incredibly gifted man who at one point lost his confidence and his way. In this story God has big plans for him, and yet Moses has become content with much less than what God has planned. God wants Moses to deliver the nation of Israel from captivity in Egypt, but Moses is content herding his father-in-law's sheep in Midian. He had tried the whole "deliverer" thing once before, and it didn't go very well.

When God shows up once again and calls him to go back to Egypt and deliver his people, immediately he begins to offer excuses for why he is unable to answer this call. During their dialogue Moses says he can't go because the people won't listen to him. At this point God asks Moses a somewhat puzzling question, "What is that in thine hand?" (Exodus 4:2).

Moses happens to be holding the rod he uses to shepherd his sheep. In essence it's a long stick used to guide the sheep and protect them in the event they're attacked by some type of wild animal. What happens next is truly amazing. Moses is instructed to throw the rod on the ground, where God turns it into a snake. God later uses the same stick and performs the very same miracle in the presence of Pharaoh. Moses strikes the Nile with the rod, and all the water in Egypt turns to blood. The rod is used to bring forth frogs from the bodies of water in Egypt. When the rod is waved over the land, lice come from the dust to plague Pharaoh and his people. Moses lifts up the rod, and the Red Sea parts. Moses hits a rock in the wilderness, and rivers of water flow and satisfy the thirst of the dehydrated Israelites. This rod is used to perform some of the most incredible things ever recorded.

Please don't lose sight of the fact that it's just *a stick*! In and of itself there is nothing special or unique about it. It's no different from a stick you might pick up during a walk in the woods, with one huge exception. After Moses runs out of excuses and answers God's call to deliver Israel from bondage, he packs up his family and starts the journey back to Egypt. "And Moses took his wife and his sons, and set them upon an ass, and he returned to the land of Egypt: and Moses took *the rod of God* in his hand" (Exodus 4:20). Did you notice anything unusual in that verse? The ordinary stick that Moses uses to herd sheep has now become "the rod of God." Moses had taken the resources he had in his hand (a stick) and had given it to God. In the hand of Moses it was nothing more than a long piece of a dead tree, but in the hand of God it was a miracle-working rod used to deliver millions of people from bondage.

God's question to us is the same one He asked Moses, "What's in your hand?" Or thinking back to our original story, He might ask, "What's in your lunch?" Each of us has something to offer God. Maybe you're an athlete of some type—give it to the Lord and watch Him work. Maybe you have business acumen—use it to turn a profit for God's glory. Maybe you're a gifted teacher—find a way to use that to instruct the body of Christ. Maybe you're a gifted craftsman and builder—use your skills to build up the body of Christ. The list of abilities and gifts that can be used in service of our King is manifold. The point is to give God the resources you have at your disposal. This applies to your abilities or gifts. This applies to your finances. This applies to your time. You may view your contribution as insignificant and therefore refrain from offering it to the Lord, but God has a different view. Take your seemingly meager gifts and place them at the disposal of your miracle-working Savior. God is in the business of using fish sandwiches and sticks to change the world. The needs of thousands were met because a little boy gave his lunch to Jesus. Millions of people were delivered from bondage because Moses allowed God to use the stick he had in his hand.

Always remember that God has the ability to take our limited resources and use them in limitless ways.

## YOUR LIFE PARABLE

1. Which approach best describes the way you have lived life in the past—wasted life, selfish life, generous life, or sacrificial life?

2. In what way(s) is God asking you to get involved in His miraculous work of taking the gospel to the world?

3. God has the ability to take your limited resources and use them in limitless ways. What seemingly insignificant gift do you possess that God could leverage to change the world? What's in your hand?

# 4

## The Instructions of Life

***Building our life upon the clear instructions of God's Word.***

I stood in the middle of the home improvement aisle at Walmart in a trance-like state. My palms started to sweat, and a cold chill crept up my spine. A warm wave of nausea began to well up in my stomach. My heart was racing, and I could feel each beat in my ears. I was an absolute mess! Was I having a heart attack? Did I have a sudden outbreak of the flu? Was it something I ate for dinner? No. This sudden eruption had been brought on by two words printed in big red letters on the side of the box directly in front of me: **ASSEMBLY REQUIRED**.

Those who know me well know that I'm not the handiest person in the world. That's a mild understatement. My wife actually throws a celebration whenever I change a light bulb around the house. However, this assembly-required panic attack wasn't brought on solely by my inability to skillfully handle a hammer and screwdriver. My assembly phobia goes far beyond any deficiency I may possess in the art of craftsmanship. There's no doubt that my lack of handyman skills leads to nervousness when I have to assemble something or make the most minor repairs around the house, but my very real fear can be traced back to an incident that occurred in the first year of our married life.

It was our first Christmas together as a married couple. We'd been married for about five glorious months. We were together in our new home, and I wanted to make this Christmas incredibly special. I was going for the real-life Hallmark moment. For months I contemplated what I should buy her—diamond earrings, a diamond bracelet, or maybe a cruise to somewhere warm and exotic? I had to get her a gift that was worthy of such an occasion; something she would never forget. Well, I got the "never forget" part right but not for the reasons you might expect.

As I mentioned, we were newlyweds in a new home, and as a result funds were limited. As recent college grads with meager means, we had mostly hand-me-down furniture in our home. As I pondered my gift purchase for Kerrie, the practical side of my brain kicked in. (Men, keep in mind that "practical" is always bad when purchasing a gift for a female.) I suddenly realized that I had a great opportunity before me. Christmas was providing me with the potential of killing two birds with this one awesome gift purchase. We had received a number of very nice gifts for our wedding—a TV, fine china, glassware, a blender, a wok, and a really nice heavy- duty microwave. The problem was that our small ranch-style house had very limited counter space. We needed somewhere to put our microwave. What we needed was a microwave cart!

Let's be honest, nothing says, "I love you" like a gift with the word *cart* in it. There's nothing quite as romantic as kitchen furniture. It's right up there with diamond jewelry or anything from Victoria's Secret. I wondered, "Where does one buy a microwave cart?" Walmart, of course. So I headed out to buy a cart for Kerrie. I found my way to the home furnishings section and started to peruse the endless array of microwave carts. They had every shape, size, and color imaginable. After several minutes of deliberating over my purchase, I decided to spare no expense and loaded up the priciest cart they had ($99). I headed to the checkout line, beaming with pride and justifying my extravagance with the thought that it was our first Christmas together and she was worth every penny. There was no doubt about it; in my mind, I was the last of the true romantics!

On Christmas morning we rolled out of bed before dawn like two small children eager to see what Santa had left them under the tree. We were filled with the excitement of experiencing our first Christmas as husband and wife. The Christmas tree filled the house with the scent of pine and gloriously mixed with the aroma of the freshly ground coffee brewing in the coffee pot (another wedding gift). The gifts were organized beneath the tree in a way that would have made Norman Rockwell proud. This was going to be epic—one of those life moments you cherish for years to come. Honestly, I don't remember any of the gifts that were given or received that morning with the exception of "the cart." I was so excited for Kerrie to see how practical and thoughtful I had been with my gift purchase.

Finally, the time had come for Kerrie to open my gift. I had intentionally saved it for last. It was going to be the grand finale to this magnificent Christmas morning. She sat on the floor next to the extremely large package and wonder filled her eyes. She slowly and neatly removed the paper from the box and paused as the contents were revealed by the large picture on the side of the cardboard box. Her wonder turned to shock. My wife is the sweetest, most godly woman I know, and she handled this atrocity with class, love, and tenderness. She never said one cruel word—at least not to my face. She simply smiled and said, "Thank you." She even gave me a peck on the cheek. In hindsight, she should have given me a right cross to the jaw.

Needless to say, I was feeling pretty good about myself. This husband thing wasn't as hard as everyone made it out to be. Filled with newfound confidence, I decided to launch into the assembly-required portion of my fabulously practical purchase. After all, how hard could it be to put together a microwave cart? Looking back on this event, I think of that verse in Proverbs that says, "Pride goeth before destruction, and an haughty spirit before a fall" (16:18). My confidence (arrogance) was about to be destroyed. I was about to be brought crashing to the ground. I tore into the box, removed all the pressed-wood pieces, retrieved the necessary tools, and promptly tossed aside the directions. After all, who needs those stinkin' directions? Right, guys?

As it turns out, *I* did. I thought things were going pretty well. I had assembled about three quarters of the cart when I realized that I had used the wrong piece of "wood" in the very first step. I had to back out all the screws and start over. At this point any reasonable person would have realized the error of his ways and quickly consulted the directions for the proper procedures in the assembly of said cart. Not me. I aimlessly dove back into the project more determined than ever to do it my own way. I was a bright young man with a college degree. I didn't need a set of juvenile directions telling me how to put Board A together with Screw B. Once again, after a sizable portion of the cart had been reassembled I realized that I had again used the wrong piece at the wrong time. The only course of action was to disassemble the entire cart for a second time. After hours of assembling, disassembling, and reassembling this stupid cart, my Christmas cheer had turned to Scrooge-like bitterness and frustration. It was so bad that I was now reduced to glancing at the directions when my wife, who kept poking her head in the kitchen and asking if I was all right, wasn't looking.

After several hours of intense assembling and disassembling the cart, I finally secured the last screw with a Grinch-like growl. The project was finally complete but with one minor problem. Repeatedly screwing and unscrewing our top-of-the-line pressed-wood microwave cart had stripped all the screw holes and left the cart looking like the Leaning Tower of Pisa. Not only did it lean, but it also swayed from side to side like a Weeble—wobbling but not falling down. It was so unstable I couldn't bring myself to put our brand new microwave on top of the Wobbling Cart of Nelson. I knew the slightest bump would bring the entire structure crashing to the floor. To my shame, I actually had to go out a few days after Christmas and purchase another cart and pay to have it assembled. All this was because I refused to follow the very simple instructions that had been provided. Thus began my assembly-required phobia and a newfound appreciation for reading and following the directions.

### *THE WOBBLY LIFE*

The Wobbling Cart of Nelson is a metaphor for the life lived in ignorance of, or with disregard for, God's very clear instructions. Trying to assembly a microwave cart, or any other assembly-required item, without consulting the directions is not dissimilar to the way we often try to conduct the business of life. Try as we may, we consistently find ourselves making huge mistakes and being forced to backtrack and start over. It doesn't take many misguided steps to cause our life to become a big wobbly mess, seemingly unfit to be used for its designed purpose. If only life came with a set of directions we could follow! The reality is that we do have instructions to follow—but we often just choose to ignore them and put our lives together in our own way. Because of pride, we think we can figure it out on our own and as a result make a conscious decision to set aside God's instructions.

At the end of the Sermon on the Mount, Jesus uses a metaphor to illustrate the key to avoiding a wobbly Christian life. In Jesus' story He mentions two men: a wise man and a foolish man. These two men had a few things in common. First, both were in the process of building a house. These houses represent two lives. Having a home is an indication of success. A home shows that we're stable. A home is a place of security. A house is the perfect metaphor for what we all strive to achieve in life—success, stability, and security. Secondly, both of these men experienced a devastating storm that threatened to destroy what they were building. These storms represent trials, troubles, or adversity in life. No one has a storm-free existence. We all experience struggles in life that sometimes shake us to our core. We cannot escape the storms of life. One of three things is true of everyone who is reading this book—you've already been through a life storm, you're currently going through a life storm, or you will someday go through a life storm. Storms are a given. How we weather the storms is the variable. Thirdly, both men heard very clear instructions from the wise master builder. There is no doubt about what they were hearing. The instructions were not vague or cloaked in mystery. Given the nature of Jesus' metaphor, we might say the men had the architect's blueprints for building their respective homes. The question was whether they would pay attention to the plans before them. But this is where the similarities stop.

These men experienced the same battering effects of the storm, but their houses emerged in two totally different states—one destroyed and one stronger than ever. Why was one sturdy and the other wobbly? Let's read the passage and see if we can discern the key elements necessary for a rock-solid life. "Therefore whosoever heareth these sayings of mine, and doeth them, I will liken him unto a wise man, which built his house upon a rock: And the rain descended, and the floods came, and the winds blew, and beat upon that house; and it fell not: for it was founded upon a rock. And every one that heareth these sayings of mine, and doeth them not, shall be likened unto a foolish man, which built his house upon the sand: And the rain descended, and the floods came, and the winds blew, and beat upon that house; and it fell: and great was the fall of it" (Matthew 7:24–27).

Did you pick up on the key difference between the foolish man and the wise man? It was the foundations they laid. The foolish man built his house on a foundation of sand, and as a result his structure was washed away when the storms came. On the other hand, the wise man built his house on a foundation of rock, and it was able to withstand the storms without falling. On the surface, during the calm, both houses looked good, and their foundations seemed sufficient. During the storms of life the inadequacy of one foundation and the strength of the other were revealed. Trials have a way of revealing the structural integrity of your life's foundation. Any structure will stand when life is peaceful and calm, but how often does that happen?

The foundation is the key to any structure that is being built. Why was one man's foundation sand and the other's rock? The text says that both men heard Jesus' sayings, but one man applied the words and the other ignored the words. Don't miss this! Both men had the necessary information required to build a house on a firm foundation, but only one of them applied the information and experienced transformation. Let's break it down this way: *application* of *information* leads to *transformation*, whereas *information* without *application* leads to *destruction*.

It's never enough to hear the necessary information. You have to be willing to apply the information to your situation. It's the application of truth that brings stability. When I put together that microwave cart, I had all the necessary information at my disposal, but I wasn't applying it. As a result I ended up with a wobbly mess. Had I taken the information provided and applied it to my situation, I would have seen the pieces of pressed wood transformed into an unshakeable and stable microwave cart.

Christians are often guilty of thinking information is enough. We deceive ourselves into thinking that if we know more facts about Jesus and God, then we are becoming more rooted and grounded in our faith and that we have stability that will carry us through the storms of life. James admonishes us, "But be ye doers of the word, and not hearers only, deceiving your own selves" (James 1;22). Application of information results in stabilization. Information without application results in self-deception. When we know a lot of facts about God but make no effort to apply it to our lives, we fool ourselves into thinking we're something we're not.

That possibility scares me to death! Have I exchanged *knowing about God* for truly *knowing God*? Have I deceived myself into thinking that I'm stronger spiritually than I really am? There's no doubt that we need information. If we don't know what God's Word says, how can we apply it to our lives? However, God didn't call us to become experts at Bible trivia or to memorize a laundry list of facts about Him. He has called us to live out what we know. He wants us to hear (or read) and then do. He wants us to apply His truth to our lives. Knowing information about God won't equip you to endure when the storms of life come. It's only through truly knowing Him that we obtain the stability and strength necessary to weather the storms. An intimate relationship with God only comes through the application of God's truth to your life.

## *THE COMPLETE LIFE*

"All scripture is given . . . that the man of God may be perfect, throughly furnished unto all good works" (2 Timothy 3:16–17). In this passage Paul tells us that one of God's purposes for humans is to be perfect and equipped to a life filled with good works. The word *perfect* as used in this passage doesn't mean "without error." It means "complete." God has given us the Scriptures so that we can become a complete followers of Him. That's a lofty goal but one that's attainable by those who are willing to follow God's clear instructions. As followers of Jesus we can experience a completed life if we're willing to allow God to fully equip us ("throughly furnish" us) through His Word.

In part, God has given us the Bible as the inspired instruction manual for life. "All scripture is given by inspiration of God, and is profitable for doctrine, for reproof, for correction, for instruction in righteousness" (2 Timothy 3:16). Our assembly-required lives don't work well without following God's instruction manual. We can try to muddle through without the instructions, but our lives will never be all that God intends without following the directions. I'm being a bit kind with that last sentence. Usually when we try to do life apart from the very clear instructions of God, we end up with a colossal mess and never come close to being complete.

According to 2 Timothy 3:16, God's Scripture has a four-fold purpose in the life of mankind. First, God's instructions are profitable for doctrine. The word *doctrine* means "teaching" or "instruction." God's first purpose for scripture is to teach us what's right. Throughout life we have a myriad of teachers—parents, school teachers, family members, friends, bosses, and so on. Some of the instruction they give is good, but, frankly, some of it is bad. The Bible shows us what is right, and we can be absolutely confident that the instructions it provides are without error. The directions the Bible provides sometimes go against what we believe to be right or what we've been taught by our other life instructors, but we must come to realize that God's thoughts are not our thoughts and His ways are not our ways. The Bible has a proven track record of infallibility, and we would do well to strive to follow its instructions.

Not only does the Bible teach us what's right, but it also shows us what's wrong. This is what the passage means when it says that the Bible is "profitable . . . for reproof." Through the Bible, God reproves His followers and shows them when they're heading the wrong direction. God doesn't reprove us because He's a great cosmic killjoy but because, as the Creator of life, He understands how life works best. God wants us to experience the complete benefits of life, and He knows we cannot do this if we're heading the wrong direction. He uses His Word and the conviction of the Holy Spirit to reprove us. Generally speaking, we don't like to be reproved or told we're doing something in an incorrect manner. It makes us angry, and we become defiant when someone points out the error of our ways. Let me encourage you to stop for a second and think. Set aside your pride, and look at this objectively. If you were driving your car down a road, and the bridge was out up ahead, wouldn't you want someone to stop you and tell you that you were heading toward danger? Of course, you would. Why is it any different when God's Word warns us that the path we are heading down is full of pitfalls? God loves, and therefore He reproves.

Not only does God show us what's right and what's wrong, but when we find ourselves heading the wrong direction, His Word shows us how to get straightened out. He shows us how to get back on the right track. This is what the passage means when it says Scripture was "given . . . for correction." In life, there is no shortage of people who will *tell* you what's right and what's wrong, but very rarely will someone care enough to *show* you how to get right. I love this about God! He not only tells me when I'm heading the wrong direction, but He cares enough to help me get back on track. When we purchase an item that requires assembly, it typically comes with step-by-step assembly instructions. If we follow the provided steps, the result will be a completed project we can be proud of. I understand that life isn't quite that neat and tidy. Fixing a broken life is rarely a matter of following a dozen easy steps in the right sequence. However, God's Word will help us make the necessary course corrections when we start to deviate from the right path. It will show us how to replace our old way of life with a new way of thinking and acting.

Building our lives in the way God intends is an ongoing process that will continue until the Lord chooses to take us home. For that reason God uses His Word to give us "instruction in righteousness." Our old sinful nature will continually tug at us and draw us off course. As a result, we need the instruction of the Bible to show us how to stay right. God trains us through Scripture so that we can live a righteous life for His glory. Even the world's most accomplished individuals need instruction. The world's greatest athlete needs a coach. The most gifted musician has a teacher. The foremost authorities in academia require training to stay abreast of the latest developments in their fields. As followers of Jesus we never arrive at a point in our walk where we no longer require instruction. God is continuously molding us and shaping us into the people He desires us to become. His Word instructs us in the right way of living.

When I purchased that top-of-the-line microwave cart, the picture on the box showed me what it was supposed to look like when it was assembled. That picture was a model and a goal. It showed me what it could look like and gave me something to strive for. God has given us a picture on the box of life. He has provided us with a model and a goal to strive for. God's picture or model is Jesus. He did life the way God intends it to be done. He was the complete ("perfect") person. He lived the perfect life by flawlessly following the instructions of His Father. As His followers, we now strive to live a life conformed to Jesus' image (Romans 8:29). He's the picture on the box we hope to one day be like. We'll never reach our goal of being like the Word, Jesus, if we aren't willing to follow God's Word, the Bible. The instructions are available to all, but it's our choice to obey them or ignore them. Allow God to build your life through His Word.

### *DO THE INSTRUCTIONS STILL WORK?*

How can a set of instructions written thousands of years ago still help us with our modern-day problems? That's a fair question—one that I myself asked when contemplating the role of the Bible in my life. After all, it would seem that people in biblical times didn't have to deal with the same types of things hounding us today. However, at their core, the struggles of modern man are no different from the struggles of mankind in the times of Jesus—or Adam for that matter. Our problems may be wrapped in a different package, but underneath they stem from the same source. We may be more technologically advanced than those living in biblical times, but our struggles are very similar. We're often guilty of mistaking advancements in technology for advancements in human nature. The Bible, though it was written thousands of years ago, still provides perfect instructions for living life to its fullest. One of the reasons you can be confident that God wrote the Bible is because it contains truth that is timeless. The prophet Isaiah had it right when he said, "Thy counsels of old are faithfulness and truth" (Isaiah 25:1). God's Word is faithful and true in spite of its age. Whether you write with a chisel and stone tablet or with your finger on the latest touch screen tablet, God's Word is applicable to your life because it deals with matters of the human heart that haven't changed since the beginning of time.

### *HOW DO YOU READ THE INSTRUCTIONS?*

Have you ever noticed that instructions for most assembly-required products seem to make the simplest tasks incredibly difficult to understand? I admit I'm not handy, but I do have a college degree, and yet reading these instructions is equivalent to reading an unknown tongue. I sometimes wonder if I'm reading the wrong language portion of the instructions.

Have you ever felt that way about the Bible? Do we need an advanced degree to comprehend the Bible's instruction? While there are certainly benefits to having an education, understanding the Bible is more about attitude than aptitude. If we come to Scripture with the right heart attitude, God will instruct us from His Word. Notice King David's attitude: "Show me thy ways, O Lord; teach me thy paths. Lead me in thy truth, and teach me: for thou art the God of my salvation; on thee do I wait all the day" (Psalm 25:4–5). One of the life lessons I continually try to impress on my kids is to always be teachable or coachable. I want them to always have a heart that is soft and ready to be instructed whether at school, in athletics, at home, and especially in response to God's Word. If we come to Scripture with a heart that desires to be instructed, God will reveal His ways to us through the work of the Holy Spirit.

Not only does God give us the instructions, but He gives us a guide, in the person of the Holy Spirit, to help us understand His instruction. The

Holy Spirit is the great teacher. He helps us interpret God's instructions. "Howbeit when he, the Spirit of truth, is come, he will guide you into all truth" (John 16:13). This is like having your very own handyman to give instruction and help you around the house with repairs and assembly.

What kept me from looking at the assembly instructions for the microwave cart so many years ago? Was it pride, stupidity, naivety, fear, testosterone? I don't really know. What I do know is that it would have been much easier if I had looked at the instructions in the first place. Had I trusted and followed what they said, I would have saved myself a lot of time, frustration, and money (because I ended up having to buy a new cart). A life is obviously much more valuable than a pressed-wood microwave cart. Therefore, it deserves to be done right. The only way to do it right is to go to the instruction manual, seeking guidance from the author. Allow the great teacher to show you how to live life His way.

As a pastor, I frequently encounter people who truly desire to follow God and live out His Word but who struggle with consistently reading and applying the Bible. They don't struggle because of limited mental capacity or because they lack advanced education in theology. Their struggles are simply the result of having never been taught how to interact with God through His Word. The purpose of this chapter (and this book) is not to give a thorough explanation for how to experience quality time in God's Word. (There are a multitude of fabulous books that can help you in that area.) But let me take a moment to give you a few tips on how you can have a more meaningful time reading God's instruction manual for life.

### *(1) READ IT DAILY.*

When we have an important appointment of some type, we block time out of our calendar and schedule around that particular meeting. If it's important to us, nothing will intrude on that appointment. I think we should be just as protective of our time with God. Make daily Bible reading a priority in your life. Make an appointment with God every day, and don't let anything infringe on that scheduled time. Schedule your time with God during a part of the day when you are at your best. If you're a morning person, then meet with God in the morning. If you're a night owl, then set up an appointment for the evening hours. The key is consistency. Set a time and keep it. Maybe as you read this paragraph, you feel yourself pushing back and saying, "You don't understand my schedule. I can't afford to take that time out of my day and spend time reading the Bible. I just don't have time!" Let me assure you, if you want a quality walk with Jesus, you can't afford not to do it. You can keep going through the motions and pretend God is your priority, but until you start spending quality time with Him in His Word, you're kidding yourself. If your schedule is so jammed you can't take fifteen to thirty minutes daily to read your Bible, it may be time to take a serious look at your calendar and make some necessary cuts.

### *(2) READ IT EXPECTANTLY.*

You must come to your devotional time expecting to hear from God. Your time in God's Word isn't simply something you endure and get through. Reading God's Word shouldn't be viewed as a checklist item that we rush through so we can get on with the really important part of our day. God's Word isn't a spiritual rabbit's foot you come to and read so that you'll have a good day. The Bible is God's Word, and you must come to it with the expectation of hearing from Him. God wants to continually speak into your life. The question is, "Are we ready to hear what He has to say?" Sometimes you hear from Him after reading one verse. Sometimes He speaks after an extended time reading His Word. The length of your reading doesn't really matter. What does matter is when He speaks, stop and listen. Bible reading plans are great tools that are meant to help us stay on track with our daily reading, but we must never exchange working through a reading plan for God working on you as you read His plan.

### *(3) READ IT PRAYERFULLY.*

Every spring and fall I plant grass seed in the bare spots in my yard. If I want the sowing of this seed to be fruitful, I must take time to prepare the soil to receive the seed. I can't simply throw the seed on the compacted, sunbaked ground. I have to turn the soil over and make it ready to receive the seed. If the soil is prepared, there's a greater likelihood grass will spring up in the spots where the seed has been sown. In a similar fashion, the soil of your heart must be prepared to receive the seed of God's Word. If you haven't taken time to prepare your heart, God may speak, but you'll receive no clear instruction.

I use a shovel and a hoe to prepare the soil in my yard, but how do you go about preparing your heart to receive God's Word? The primary tool for preparing your heart is prayer. It can be something as simple as this prayer offered by David: "Open thou mine eyes, that I may behold wondrous things out of thy law" (Psalm 119:18). Remember that heart attitude is the key. Prepare your heart to meet with God as you read your Bible. Don't rush into God's presence. Still yourself through prayer. Prepare your heart by asking God to cleanse you and meet with you. Stilling your heart before the Lord has a way of opening your ears so you can receive His clear instructions.

### *(4) READ IT PREEMPTIVELY.*

I'm a diligent daily vitamin taker. Every day I take a handful of vitamins that are supposedly providing my body with the nutrients necessary for it to function properly. I also occasionally take ibuprofen to help counter the effects of a headache or other body ache. The vitamin is preventative, and the ibuprofen is more immediate. The Bible is better taken as a vitamin than as ibuprofen. It will work as a pain reliever for whatever ails you, but a wiser approach is to read it for the purpose of building and strengthening your life. Many people only come to God's Word when they're in crisis. They randomly open the Bible, stab their finger into a page, and hope they find an answer in the verse under their extended digit. I'm not saying you can't receive some relief from your pain by employing this method, but I'm sure it's not the most effective approach. We shouldn't just come to the Bible when we have a problem. Store up for the time of need. God knows what problems you'll encounter in the future, and He can use His Word to help prepare you now to face those issues when they do come your way.

### *(5) READ IT PERSONALLY.*

God wrote the Bible for you. It contains personalized instructions for your life. We must keep this in mind; otherwise, it's very easy to fall into the trap of reading the Bible in a detached manner. This results in a very dry interaction with the Bible. I fully acknowledge that some portions of the Bible are more exciting than others. However, all of it is God's Word and can benefit those who are willing to read and receive its instructions. Some of the biggest blessings I've received from God's Word are in obscure passages in Leviticus, Numbers, Judges, and Habakkuk (yes, that's actually a book in the Bible). One thing that can make the Bible come alive is to put yourself into the narrative. How would you have responded in certain situations? What would have been going through your mind? The characters in Scripture were real people with emotions, doubts, and fears just like you. Interact with the narrative by placing yourself in the story.

Twenty-five years ago God taught me an incredibly valuable life lesson for the inexpensive price of $99 for a wobbly microwave cart and a few frustrating hours of my time. All things considered, I got off cheap because I learned a valuable truth that I've carried with me for the past two and a half decades—read and follow the instructions! Maybe the price you've paid to learn this same lesson has been much higher—a broken marriage, mistakes raising your kids, misguided financial decisions, a life of addiction, or a purposeless existence. Whatever price you've paid and wherever you now find yourself, God's Word can help you reconstruct your life and give you the stability we all long for. I know it's difficult to admit you need help, but it's time for you to stop trying to figure life out on your own and to start reading and following God's clear instructions. Open up the Bible, and let God show you how to construct a beautiful life for His honor and glory.

## YOUR LIFE PARABLE

1) In what area(s) of your life have you disregarded God's clear instructions? What was the result?

2) Develop and implement a daily plan for reading God's Word.

3) We read the Bible not only to be informed but to be transformed. The key to our transformation is application. As you daily interact with God in His Word, look for a take-away truth that can be applied to your life.

# 5

## The Wheel of Life

***Managing our resources for God's glory.***

The clatter from downstairs woke me out of a dead sleep. The newest addition to our family was at it again. Since our family was well past the newborn years, at first I thought I was dreaming. But as I gingerly made my way toward the kitchen, there was no denying the little one was awake. My wife, without my permission, had brought him home from her classroom at the end of the school year. He had only been a part of our household for a few days, but he was making his presence known in a mighty way. How could something so small make such a racket? Entering the kitchen, I glanced at the clock on the microwave. It read 3:07—time to have a little man-to-rodent talk with Huey the Hamster.

As I peered into Huey's cage, I found myself fighting back thoughts of how I might dispose of him before my kids awoke—a ride on the toilet bowl express, setting him free in the neighborhood so the neighbor's cat could have a little snack, or even a Lenny-like squeeze. My malicious thoughts were quickly replaced with fascination as I became mesmerized by his incessant activity. Knowing I would be unable to go back to sleep, I pulled up a chair and watched as the fuzzy little brown-and-white creature scurried about in his world. He would run over to his food dish and eat. Then he would rush over and get a drink from the silver tube hanging on his wall. From there he would dash into his little home and hide some food in the straw that lined the cage. Finally, he would scurry to his wheel and run at top speed (and sound) for minutes at a time. This pattern repeated itself for as long as I could bear to watch. Huey's life consisted of three major activities: taking nourishment (eating and drinking), sleeping (which he did during the day), and running on his wheel (which he did *all* night long). Day after day, week after week, Huey scampers through the trio of activities that comprise and define his existence. It's a simple and almost sad existence but one that he has grown accustomed to. In fact, you might say that Huey doesn't really know any other way to operate. He would be lost in any other environment. It's the only life he has ever known.

At some point during this encounter, I was struck by the similarity between my existence and that of Huey the Hamster. Broken down to its most basic form, my life consists of three primary functions: taking nourishment; sleeping; and running on my wheel. Huey may be content and comfortable with this life, but I often find myself longing for more. Food, drink, and sleep are necessities of life. Our bodies need fuel, and they need a proper amount of rest. If we neglect these basic need areas, we eventually do ourselves harm. However, for most people it's the "wheel running" that causes the most serious trouble. Why is this? Just as a finely tuned automobile that continually runs at dangerously high RPMs will eventually break down, so too our bodies will ultimately break down physically if we incessantly push them to extremes. However, the main problem with the frantic pace of life is that it robs me of the life-giving connection with my heavenly Father. The wheel of life, whether because of speed or noise, inhibits my ability to relate to God. Often I'm in such a hurry to get somewhere, be something, or impress someone that I have no time for God, who might as well be left spinning in the backwash from my wheel. Relationships can't be built while moving at breakneck speed. Relationship requires time, stillness, intentionality, and focus; all of which are nonexistent when I'm on the wheel.

After pastoring for several decades, I'm convinced that the sin that so easily besets most followers of Jesus is not one of the overt sins such as addiction, sexual promiscuity, pornography, greed, or materialism. Which sin causes us to stumble and become dry in our walk with God? Busyness! The hurried lifestyle is one of the major killers of spiritual vitality in the twenty-first century. In his book, *The Life You've Always Wanted*, John Ortberg refers to this epidemic as "hurry-sickness." We are speed junkies. We're addicted to adrenaline. There's no question that life in the fast lane is fascinating, even addictive, but sooner or later it leads down a road that plunges over the edge of a cliff. Or worse yet, it can result in a person just spinning his wheels and missing out on the abundant life found in Christ. We exchange a filled calendar for the full life. We settle for action when God wants us to experience transformation. As I mentioned earlier, the most costly effect of our frantic pace in life is loss of relationship. At the end of our time here on earth, we won't regret not spending enough time at the office or long to have been involved in more meaningless activities. We will wish we had spent more time relating to those we love most.

When I was a kid, one of my favorite cartoons centered on the exploits of a futuristic family called the Jetsons. In the title sequence we see the main character, George Jetson, running on his space-age treadmill at an unsustainable pace. Using all his energy to keep up and stay upright, George screams the famous line to his wife, "Jane, get me off this crazy thing!" Little did I know then that George Jetson was speaking prophetically about the pace of my own life and the lives of most Christ followers in the Western world. I often find myself muttering the words of the great prophet, George Jetson, "God, get me off this crazy thing!" The question is, "How do I jump off the wheel of life, which is spinning at breakneck speed?" What can I do to reclaim the life-giving connection with my heavenly Father?

## MARTHA, MARTHA

Can you imagine having Jesus as a guest in your home? What an incredible honor and privilege to have the Son of God under your roof. We clean our home from attic to basement when our normal everyday friends come over; I can't imagine what type of cleaning my wife would have us doing if the Creator of the universe was going to stop by. What type of meal would you prepare for the one called the Bread of Life and Living Water? Italian, Mexican, Chinese, burgers? It's safe to say that whatever preparations we made and whatever meal we served, we would strive to put our best foot forward and receive Jesus in a manner befitting His stature. What if we made the grandest of preparations in anticipation of His arrival, but when He finally stopped by, we never bothered to interact with Him? We busied ourselves in the kitchen preparing drinks and food. We spent our time folding napkins and making sure the silverware was in the right order (did Jesus know which fork to use first?). All the while Jesus was in the family room talking with the other guests and giving them insight into the deepest issues of life. While there's certainly nothing wrong with attempting to serve Jesus with our very best effort, we must never be so burdened with busyness that we forego the opportunity to sit at the feet of Jesus and learn from Him. This is exactly what happened when Jesus visited Martha and Mary.

"Now it came to pass, as they went, that he entered into a certain village: and a certain woman named Martha received him into her house. And she had a sister called Mary, which also sat at Jesus' feet, and heard his word. But Martha was cumbered about much serving, and came to him, and said, Lord, dost thou not care that my sister hath left me to serve alone? bid her therefore that she help me. And Jesus answered and said unto her, Martha, Martha, thou art careful and troubled about many things: But one thing is needful: and Mary hath chosen that good part, which shall not be taken away from her" (Luke 10:38–42).

Martha was running on the wheel of busyness, whereas Mary was being still at the feet of Jesus. Because of her incessant activity, Martha was experiencing self-pity, fatigue, worry, anxiety, and relational disconnect. Mary, on the other hand, had chosen the one thing that is needful and good. She was spending time connecting with Jesus and being blessed in a way that could never be taken away from her. The activity of Martha wasn't necessarily sinful, but she had allowed less important things to jump in front of the one needful thing—connection with Jesus. This happens all the time in our lives. We aren't engaged in overt sin, but we have misplaced our priorities and allowed less important things to rob us of our life-giving connection with God. As a result of her busyness, Martha's relationship with Jesus is hindered, and her relationship with her sister, Mary, is suffering. Martha demonstrates our inability to build relationships, earthly or heavenly, while focused on maintaining the busyness of life. When hurry or busyness defines our lives, we will be filled with anxiety and worry. Fatigue will eventually overcome us, and we'll break down physically, emotionally, and spiritually. Our focus will be on self, and when that happens, we can't build relationships with others or with God. Obviously, God never intended for us to live in such a state.

As I thought about Huey, Martha, and my life, God began to reveal to me the steps I needed to take in order to get off my wheel, or at least to slow it down to a more sustainable speed. It became evident that three huge paradigm shifts were necessary in my life.

### *UNDERSTAND I AM ACCOUNTABLE*

For a moment imagine that you're the latest huge lottery winner. As a result of holding the winning ticket, $86,400 will be deposited into your bank account each day for the rest of your life—let's hope you're thirty rather than ninety—but there's a catch. You're not allowed to carry over any of the $86,400 to the next day. In other words, what you don't spend you lose, and you can never get it back. You'll receive a fresh amount each day, but the unspent amount from the previous day is gone forever. Having this arrangement would most likely lead to one of two extreme approaches to handling the money. We would either be exceptionally diligent in managing, or spending, our daily allotment of dollars, by making sure our bank account balance was zero at the end of each day; or, over time, we would get bored, blow off the process, and begin thinking there's always tomorrow and another $86,400. Be honest, which scenario would be true of you? As weird as it sounds, I suspect most people fall into the second group and would get bored with the process of wisely managing their funds. Eventually, they would end up wasting more money than they spent.

Every day of your life, God deposits 86,400 seconds into your time (life) bank account. Portions of your deposit are allocated for life's necessities like sleeping, eating, and watching NFL football on Sundays, but the remainder of the time is for you to use as you will. What you choose to waste is gone forever—you can never get it back once it's gone. For this reason, I believe time is our most valuable commodity. You can get more money, and you can get more possessions, but you can never get more time. Once time is gone, it is gone forever. A. W. Tozer once wrote: "Time is a resource that is nonrenewable and nontransferable. You cannot store it, slow it up, hold it up, divide it up or give it up. You can't hoard it up or save it for a rainy day—when it's lost its unrecoverable. When you kill time, remember that it has no resurrection."

God has given us the unbelievable gift of life which is composed of time. The question before us is how we're going to use it. Does the knowledge that we have limited time drive us to heightened diligence, or do we grow bored with the process? Do we begin to think there's always tomorrow and therefore start to blow off today's possibilities? The problem with that way of thinking is that we aren't guaranteed tomorrow. Benjamin Franklin said, "Do not squander time, for it is the stuff life is made of." Young or old, none of us can be certain we're going to receive a fresh set of 86,400 seconds tomorrow. Therefore, we need to take advantage of the time we have been given today.

As I contemplated slamming on the brakes of my wheel, the first thing I realized was that I am a steward of the things God has given me, including my most precious commodity: time. How I utilize the time I've been given is my decision, but I must understand that one day I will give an account to my heavenly Father for how I have invested the time given to me on earth. I only have life (time) because He allows it to be so. All time is in His hand. Only God knows how much time we have on this earth. My life is literally in His hands, and I am responsible to Him for how I utilize the time He has given me. The question I must ask myself is, "How am I investing my daily allotment of 86,400 seconds?" As I examined my life I came to the conclusion that if I were a stockbroker, making financial investments, I would have been fired long ago. At that point, I decided to heed the admonition of Ephesians 5:16 and Colossians 4:5 and redeem my time.

When we approach time investments from the standpoint of being a steward, it makes every scheduling decision a God decision. Have you ever thought of your calendar as a spiritual document? Most likely not; but that's exactly what it is when you turn it over to God and start making decisions based on Him and His desires. The contemplation of scheduling decisions becomes a question of wisdom rather than simple availability. Instead of asking, "Can I fit this in?" I begin to ask, "Does God want me to fit this in?" When I realize I am a manager of God's time, my calendar becomes spiritual in nature. It helps me to understand that my life is not my own (1 Corinthians 6:19–20; Romans 12:1). The decision to get out of ownership and into management helps me become a better manager of the resources at my disposal.

### *MAKING GOD MY PRIORITY*

Our family calendar is truly something to behold. It's almost like a piece of art. Each of the four people has a color assigned to designate his or her particular events. I'm green, my wife is yellow, my son is purple, and my daughter is red. Each month is a new brightly colored kaleidoscope of appointments, meetings, and events displayed on our smartphones, tablets, computers, and refrigerator. I enter my personal items into my Outlook calendar, which syncs with my Google calendar, which combines with our family calendar, and out pops the agenda for the month. Our family is very intentional about scheduling items that are important to us. Why? So we don't double book or forget something important. If you call me and try and schedule a meeting, the first thing I'll do is check the calendar. If there is something important already in that time slot, then we're going to have to find another date and time. The bottom line is this: if it's important, it gets scheduled and ends up on the calendar.

This raises the question, "Why aren't we as protective of and conscientious with our God time? If we say that God is our number-one priority in life, why isn't He scheduled into our calendars? I see business meetings, soccer games, date nights, and school concerts but very little God Almighty. God is the one who gave us our time in the first place, and He's the only one who knows exactly how much time we have left, so doesn't it make sense that we would give Him a good portion of our time back in return? Where we spend our time says a great deal about our priorities in life. You can tell me what's important to you, but how you spend your time is the ultimate indicator of your real priorities.

Once we make the mental shift from being owners to being managers of our time, we need to get really practical. We need to take a good hard look at our calendars. When I did this in my own life, what I found spoke volumes to me about the priorities in my life. God was getting squeezed out or, at best, getting leftovers. Remember what I said earlier about a hurried lifestyle and relationships? Relationships cannot be developed when we're frantically moving through life. You don't grow in your knowledge of God when you're continually trying to squeeze Him in to your already too-full calendar. We have to become more intentional about our time with God in His Word, in prayer, and in meditation. We need to treat our time with God like any other important appointment on our calendar. Block out your daily one-on-one God time in your calendar. If God truly is your priority, He should get your best time. If you wake up in the morning bright eyed and saying, "Good morning, Lord!" then schedule a morning meeting with God. If your alarm clock goes off and you say, "Good Lord, it's morning!" but you're still going strong after 10:00 p.m., then have a midnight rendezvous with Jesus. Whenever you choose to schedule your God time, make it your priority and make it non-negotiable.

There are 168 hours in each week. On average we spend 56 hours sleeping, about 24 hours on eating and personal hygiene, and 50 hours working and traveling to work. That leaves us approximately 35 hours a week (5 hours a day) of "discretionary" time to play with. If you have children, a good portion, if not the majority of your discretionary hours, are consumed by taxiing kids to and from various events, attending games and concerts, and helping little Johnny with his math homework. However large or small your pool of discretionary time may be, the question is, "Where are you investing those hours?" That's a question that you urgently need to consider.

Maintaining a daily quality time with God will help you avoid hopelessly spinning on the wheel of life. It sounds contradictory, but the busier you get, the more important it becomes to make time for God. As busy as Jesus was during His earthly ministry, He never lost sight of the need to connect with His heavenly Father. Right after one of His most famous miracles (the feeding of the five thousand), Jesus did something that I believe is very instructive for us. "And when he had sent the multitudes away, he went up into a mountain apart to pray: and when the evening was come, he was there alone" (Matthew 14:23). Jesus was continually getting pulled a thousand different directions by the demands of His ministry, and yet He was intentional about maintaining His life-giving connection with the Father. Why? He understood how crucial that relationship was to maintaining a God-honoring lifestyle. It was through that relationship that He received the spiritual nourishment and strength to carry out His mission on earth. He understood that He couldn't do what God expected of Him without staying connected to His ultimate source of power. Might I suggest, if Jesus needed it, we need it too. If your calendar is full, you must make sure your heart is filled with God's Spirit. If you don't, you'll have a filled calendar, but your life will be empty.

### *TAKING RESPONSIBILITY FOR MY LIFE*

I want you to practice with me saying one of the most difficult words in the English language. It's not an unfamiliar word; in fact, we use it all the time, but when it comes to our calendar it's a word that rarely crosses our lips. OK, here we go! Ready for it? Say it with me, "No." Try it again, "No." How'd that feel? Good, right? Even when we start thinking like managers of time rather than owners, and begin treating God as our number-one priority in life, we can still find our wheel spinning faster than we would like. We all have a tendency to get caught up in the rat (or hamster) race and flow of everyone else's frenzied life. We're trying to keep God first on our calendars, but the calendars are so filled with other activities that we often feel squeezed by the daily flow of life.

One day I had a revelation that was very simple and yet so profound. I realized that I call the shots when it comes to my schedule. I know that may sound like a very elementary concept, but we often conduct ourselves as though we're puppets that move at the beck and call of the puppeteer. If *you* don't manage your time, there's no shortage of people who will gladly handle that for you. When it comes to my wheel, I shouldn't allow others, including my kids, to dictate the speed I run at. There's no lack of opportunities for activity. In the age we live in and in the country we live in, our disposable time can get quickly gobbled up. If we will commit to this new paradigm, it will make scheduling decisions much easier. We will become better equipped to fight the tendency to overcommit to those things that detract from the true priorities of life.

Pastors often lament the lack of commitment on the part of Christians today. I strongly disagree with this sentiment. I don't believe present-day Christians lack the commitment of past generations. The problem isn't undercommitment but rather overcommitment. We're committed to our mortgage payments, our car payments, and our credit card payments and to being den mothers or youth soccer coaches, taking dance classes, watching our favorite TV programs, and the list goes on and on. When we become committed to too many things, the priority items of life lose out. When we're involved in too many things, we end up not doing any of them well, including our walk with God. Our spiritual enemy is perfectly content with us being distracted from our God-given purpose. We become ineffective when we become overly active. We become the proverbial dog chasing its tail (or hamster running on its wheel). Take responsibility for your time and make wise scheduling decisions based on the godly priorities of life. When you are faced with a scheduling opportunity, consider if it is the wise thing to do and not simply if you have time to do it. If it's not wise, then don't do it. If it is wise, then do it with all your might.

### *HURRY WITHDRAWAL*

The other day something highly unusual happened with Huey the Hamster. I actually thought he was dying. He wouldn't eat. He wouldn't drink. He spent all his time sleeping. He wasn't his normal hyperactive self. One morning I was checking in on him and happened to notice that the little house in his cage was jammed against his wheel and keeping it from spinning. He wasn't able to run on the wheel. A rather large portion of his life had been taken away. I'm no hamster psychologist, but I honestly believe that this depressed Huey. He had lost his purpose for living. If he wasn't able to run on his wheel, what was the point of living? His life was defined by his activities—eating, drinking, sleeping, and *running*!

When we attempt to jump off our wheel, or at least slow it to a manageable pace, at times it will feel as though life has lost its meaning. Why? Because, whether we realize it or not, we associate worth and purpose with activity. Our lives have become defined by the number of things we do. This is especially true for all you hard-charging type-A personalities who are reading this. When the activity stops or slows, you suffer from "hurry withdrawal." Think about the number of times you (or others around you) have answered the question, "How's it going?" with the one-word answer, "Busy!" Even if we aren't presently all that busy, we want others to think we are. Why? Because being busy means worth; achievement means acceptance; and stillness means fear.

If I'm busy, then I'm more valuable. To who? Your worth isn't defined by how many activities you can cram into a twenty-four-hour period. Having times of inactivity in your life doesn't make you less valuable. In fact, in many ways, it makes you more valuable because you become more useful to your Creator. I've come to realize that stillness creates value because it creates connection between me and my Maker. It is in those still moments of life that God can speak to us. "Be still, and know that I am God" (Psalm 46:10). At least once a year, I try to get away for a personal retreat where it's just God and me. I take my Bible, my journal, and a pen. I don't take along my laptop, my tablet, or even my phone. Inevitably, I spend the first twenty-four hours pacing around my room fidgeting like a drug addict who has been cut off. I find myself tormented by the inactivity. My body, my mind, my spirit have become so used to continual movement and stimulus that it takes them some time to unwind and reconnect with God Almighty.

We need to connect with God, but we can do that only if we're willing to create space in our lives to do so. We create space by learning to say "no" to many of the opportunities that life presents us. When it comes to our time (life), the good is the enemy of the best. In other words, when we're involved in too many "good" things the "best" things of life (God) tend to get squeezed out or receive far less than our best effort. *Less* truly is *more* when it comes to life's calendar. When we do less, we can be more effective at the things that truly matter in life.

Jumping off the wheel of life, or at least slowing it down, sounds well and good, but is it really practical? As you're reading this chapter, you may be thinking, "I don't have time for this right now!" That response is driven by fear. You think, "If I don't do as much as I can, I'll never make it." What's "it"? "I'll fall behind." Behind who or what? "I'll be poor." What is "poor"? "I won't be acceptable." To whom? "I won't measure up." To what? Are these legitimate concerns, or are they demons that drive you to run as fast as you can because you're afraid? Culture will continue to push you to the breaking point by placing demands on your time. Culture wants our life running at maximum RPMs. If we don't take steps to get this under control, eventually it will catch up to us, and we will burn out. We need to do less but do it more effectively. We need to understand that our worth is linked to the fullness of our relationship with Him, not the fullness of our calendars. We need to stop allowing the wheel of life to rob us of the life-giving connection with our heavenly Father.

## YOUR LIFE PARABLE

1) On the road to recovery, the first step always involves admitting you have a problem. Take some time right now to seek God's forgiveness for your hurry addiction. Ask His help in getting victory over this life-sucking sin.

2) Begin redeeming your time as it says in Ephesians 5:16. Change your mindset, and approach each day as a gift from God filled with opportunities. Begin each day with a simple prayer, "God use me this day to bring You honor and glory."

3) When it comes to time management (life management), the good is the enemy of the best. What good things do you need to say "no" to so you can take advantage of the Lord's best for your life?

# 6

## The Depth of Life

***Allowing abundance, awe, and abandon to define our life.***

Sweat dripped through my facemask as I bent over and placed my hands on my knees in exhaustion. The huddle looked like a gathering of chain smokers as the warm breath from our lungs wafted into the cool night air. I nervously gnawed on my peppermint mouth guard in anticipation of the next play call. Though we were still in elementary school, this was our Super Bowl—the Chargers versus the Cowboys—the championship game of the Peewee Pop Warner League.

As the quarterback, I knew everyone was looking to me to make a play and break the 0-0 tie midway through the third quarter. I relished the opportunity to make a game-changing run, win the game, and have bragging rights at school for weeks to come. The coach stepped into the huddle and gave us the play he wanted us to run, "Quarterback sweep left." This was my big chance. There was only one problem. Matt Martin was playing right cornerback for the defense of the Cowboys. Matt was a good friend of mine, and it was common knowledge that he was the fastest kid in school. Try as we might, no one in our grade could outrun Matt Martin. Needless to say, I didn't have very much confidence in the play call of the coach. I didn't think our blockers could block Matt, and I didn't think I had enough speed to get around him.

As we broke the huddle I glanced to my right and saw Mack Crowley playing left cornerback for the Cowboys. A light bulb went off in my little

Peewee brain. I stepped under center and called the cadence, "Down, set, hut one, hut two." The ball was snapped and our team moved to the left as a precisely choreographed unit. Linemen pinned their men at the line of scrimmage and sealed the left edge, receivers blocked downfield on the left side, and the running back provided a lead block around the left corner. The only problem was, the quarterback (me) didn't go left; he went right toward Mack Crowley. You see, I knew I would have no problem outrunning Mack in a footrace. The coach didn't know what I did about Matt's speed. In my opinion he had called the wrong play. We should have been going right toward Mack and away from Matt. Both teams flowed to the left side of the field and that left Mack Crowley and me, one on one, on the right side.

I don't know if I underestimated Mack's speed or overestimated my own, but either way, Mack did his best Ray Lewis impersonation and quickly tackled me behind the line of scrimmage. As I slowly walked back to the huddle trying to figure what had just happened, the coach met me halfway, bent over, looked me in the eye, and asked me if I knew my right from my left. We gathered back in the huddle, and the coach said, "OK. That was an honest mistake, but let's try this again. Quarterback sweep *left*!" Pointing in the direction he wanted me to run.

As we broke the huddle, I quickly glanced to my left and saw the speedy Matt Martin just waiting to tackle me. In my heart I once again began to question the wisdom of the coach's call. Slowly walking toward the line of scrimmage, I glanced to my right and found Mack Crowley still gloating over the last play. My blood started to boil and I was determined to put him in his place. I crouched under center and barked out the signals, "Down, set, hut one, hut two!" As if shot from a gun our entire team fired off the line and flowed to the left side of the field. The lone exception to this beautifully orchestrated movement was the guy with the ball—me! Once again, with my entire team going left, I arbitrarily decided that the best course of action was to go right. This was it— me and Mack once again one on one; may the best man win.

I've never had a clearer déjà vu moment in my life. Mack hit me with the same speed and ferocity that he did the first time. I even think it was in the exact same spot on the field. As I lay on the field in a crumpled mass, my coach sprinted to my side not to see if I was OK but to tell me to get my rear out of the game and grab some pine on the bench. As he'd watched me once again go right when I had been told to go left, he had determined that this wasn't an act of stupidity by someone who didn't know his left from his, but an act of defiance by someone who thought it was better to run right than left. Needless to say, he was not pleased. He had every right to be furious with me for openly disobeying his very clear commands. I had no excuses.

I pulled off my helmet and grabbed a seat near the end of the bench. Tears flowed down my cheeks as I placed my head in my hands and started to sob like a baby. Suddenly, the crowd of parents watching the game erupted. Their screams jarred me back to reality. I lifted my head just in time to see my replacement cross the goal line for what would be the game winning touchdown. I looked back up the field and what did I see—Matt Martin lying flat on his back with our fullback standing over him. Quarterback sweep left! It had worked. The disappointment with my own behavior and with being taken out of the game was replaced with a newfound respect for my coach. It seems he did know something that I didn't. I thought my inside knowledge of Matt and Mack's speed made me an expert on coordinating an offense. I didn't realize that the years of coaching experience had given my coach a much larger perspective than I had. What he needed from me was obedience to his command even when I didn't understand or agree with the play call.

At the time I didn't fully grasp the spiritual lessons I was learning during this Pop Warner football game. As a child, my big take-away from that event was that when the coach says go left, you go left. Years later, as I contemplated the true nature and the depth of obedience in our Christian walk, I was reminded of this childhood episode as I read in Luke 5 about an incident that occurred early in the ministry of Jesus Christ. The disciples were still getting to know Jesus. They'd spent some time with Him, and they'd been impressed with His teachings and workings to this point, but they didn't fully understand the magnitude of His person quite yet. This was evidenced by the fact that some of them were still engaged in their trade of commercial fishing. They were disciples of Jesus, but they hadn't left their day jobs. That started to change during this simple, and yet profound, encounter with the carpenter from Nazareth.

### *STAYING IN THE SHALLOWS*

Jesus was teaching a group of people near the shore of Lake Gennesaret. It was a large group of people, and everyone was pressing in close to hear what this supposed prophet had to say. As the people stepped forward and Jesus stepped back, He ran out of land and found Himself at the water's edge. A group of fishermen, including some of Jesus' disciples stood nearby washing their nets after a long night of fruitless fishing. Jesus had an idea. "And he entered into one of the ships, which was Simon's, and prayed him that he would thrust out a little from the land. And he sat down, and taught the people out of the ship" (Luke 5:3). Jesus had Peter help him create an impromptu speaking platform in the shallow waters of the lake so He could address the large group that had gathered on the shore.

The number of people gathered and the location of the speaker are not a coincidence. I believe the shallowness of the water from which Jesus speaks points to the place where many, if not most, Christians are in their relationship with Jesus. They have a shallow, superficial relationship. Richard Foster once wrote that "superficiality is the curse of our age." God doesn't want the church to be a mile wide and an inch deep. He desires for His followers to wade in over their heads and swim in the depths of an intimate relationship with Him. How do we obtain this type of depth in our relationship with Jesus? Is it through increased knowledge? Does it occur naturally over the course of time?

As a pastor, I'm often asked to teach a group the "deep" things of Scripture. There's a misconception in Western Christianity that knowledge equals depth. The more information you know about God and the Bible, the deeper you are. However, information alone doesn't bring about depth in our relationship with God. The information we have must result in application in our lives, which in turn, brings about a transformation in our hearts. We'll see this in a moment as we consider a group of guys who were asked to launch out into the deep.

Through their own choice the majority of Christians today are content to stay on the shore or in the ankle-deep water, having their ears tickled by the teachings of Jesus. There is a transfer of information, but never a transformation through application. If you are happy and comfortable in the shallow end of the pool, you should stop reading this chapter right now. If you desire to go deeper with God and experience real transformation in your life and in the lives of those around you, then put on your floaties, and let's go swimming in the deep end.

### *LAUNCHING INTO THE DEEP*

After preaching His baby-pool message to the large group gathered on the shore, Jesus turned to Peter and the other disciples in the boat and asked them to, "Launch out into the deep, and let down your nets for a draught" (Luke 5:4). He wanted them to head out into the deep water, and do a little fishing. This is no idle request. Peter and other guys had just come in from a hard night of working on the boat, and their nets had just been cleaned and put away. It was going to take them some work to get everything ready to fulfill Jesus' request. The request was counterintuitive to Peter and his crew. It went against everything Peter knew as a fisherman. Everyone knows the best time to fish is at night, and now this carpenter was telling them to launch out into the deep water in the heat of the day.

Seriously, put yourself in Peter's position in regard to this request. Imagine someone coming into your place of employment who had no experience whatsoever in your industry and telling you how to do your job. How would you receive their input? I'm pretty sure it wouldn't be well received. Peter no doubt felt a little like I did when my football coach said to go left against Matt Martin when I knew the best course of action was to go right toward Mack Crowley. Peter felt he had information and understanding that Jesus didn't know or consider. Despite his fishing acumen and hard-earned expertise when it came to catching fish, we see Peter display some humility (or is it condescension) in his response to Jesus' request. "And Simon answering said unto him, Master, we have toiled all the night, and have taken nothing: nevertheless at thy word I will let down the net" (Luke 5:5).

You've got to admit that Peter handled this pretty well given the circumstances—he'd been up all night working hard. For all his efforts he hadn't caught any fish (which meant no money), and now he had this carpenter telling them how to fish. You really couldn't blame Peter if he had thrown Jesus overboard and gone home to take a nap. At first Peter tried to help Jesus understand how silly His request was: "We have toiled all the night, and have taken nothing" (5:5). But then with one word, (*nevertheless*), he went against his instincts and gave in to the very clear command of Jesus. Peter did what I wouldn't do; he submitted himself to the person of authority in his life. I thought my coach was crazy and didn't know what he was doing. Therefore, I didn't follow through with what he asked of me. But Peter responded well to Jesus' instructions. Peter said, "At thy word, I will let down the net" (5:5). There was no doubt about what Jesus wanted him to do, just as there was no doubt about what my coach wanted me to do, "Quarterback sweep left." The issue wasn't clarity; it was obedience.

There are a few common reasons why we don't respond obediently to our Master. One is fear. We are simply afraid of what might await us, and therefore, we do nothing. Another is pride. We're arrogant about knowing how things should operate, and we're unwilling to give credence to outside input, even when the input comes from none other than Jesus. We sometimes look at Scripture and the very clear instruction it provides with arrogance, wondering how a book written thousands of years ago by guys in the Middle East could have anything worthwhile to say about our lives today. We forget that the true author is the Creator and Sustainer of life who has insights we can't possibly know or understand. We feel we know best how to live our lives and lose sight of the fact that life is at its best when it is lived in accordance with God's very clear commands. Jesus is not ambiguous about what He wants us to do and how He wants us to live. The issue isn't whether we get it, but whether we will do it.

## *DEPTH THROUGH OBEDIENCE*

Peter received his very clear instructions from Jesus. He told Jesus they were going to follow His commands even though he thought it would be a colossal waste of time. Then he followed through and actually did it. This is not a minor point. We routinely hear the clear instructions of God whether through the reading of God's word, listening to a sermon, reading our favorite Christian author, or even feeling the prompting of God's Holy Spirit within us. We regularly give God lip service by telling Him we have heard His command and will respond accordingly. The breakdown comes when it is time to follow through and actually be obedient.

In that football huddle so many years ago, I clearly understood what my coach wanted, and I gave every indication that I was going to respond accordingly. But when it came time to execute, I did the exact opposite of what was expected. Peter didn't completely understand what was going on, but he was obedient nonetheless—and look what happened: "And when they had this done, they enclosed a great multitude of fishes: and their net brake" (5:6). Peter was obedient to what Jesus had him do, and as a result he experienced a tremendous blessing.

Don't miss the connection between the blessing, Peter's obedience, and the location. Blessing occurs when we go deeper with Jesus, and going deep with Jesus results from obedience. We might say it this way, the depth of our relationship with God is determined by our level of obedience to His Word. Depth in the Christian life does not result from how much information you know about the Bible, God, or Jesus. Depth is not a function of how long you've been a Christian. Depth doesn't automatically come because you go to church every week or give a lot of money. Depth of relationship comes from application of information. In other words, it comes from obedience. It never ceases to amaze me how casually we treat God's Word. We're sometimes guilty of viewing it as on par with advice from Dr. Phil or Oprah. The Bible is the Word of God. It contains

God's directives, commands, and promises for you. It's not "chicken soup for your soul"; it's a seven-course meal that you can't live without.

Without question, one of the most convicting verses in the entire Bible is Luke 6:46, where Jesus said, "Why call ye me Lord, Lord and do not the things which I say?" How can you call him Lord of your life and yet be unwilling to obey? The answer is you can't! If He is your Lord, then you will obey Him. If you're not obeying Him, then He's not your Lord. That's not to say there won't be times of struggle or poor choices made on our part, but underneath all of that is a heart that desires to obediently follow Jesus.

### *OBEDIENT LIFE EQUALS ABUNDANT LIFE*

God desires to bless you. God wants you to experience the abundance of life (John 10:10). Abundance isn't always equated with material blessings, but it's always equated with obedience. Our abundance will be in direct proportion to our obedience. Can you imagine the look on Peter's face as he lowered his net over the side of the boat and then felt the weight grow heavy as it filled with fish? It quickly became too heavy for him and his crew to handle. He had to call out to his partners in another boat to come and give them a hand. They had toiled all night long and caught nothing, and now, after acting in obedience to Jesus' command, they experienced such an abundant haul of fish that their nets started to break, and their boat was filled to the point of beginning to sink. "And when they had this done, they enclosed a great multitude of fishes: and their net brake. And they beckoned unto their partners, which were in the other ship, that they should come and help them. And they came, and filled both the ships, so that they began to sink" (Luke 5:6–7).

Peter and his crew were almost overwhelmed by the gracious abundance they experienced from the Lord. I wonder what they would have experienced had they been completely obedient? What do I mean? Go back and look at the clear command of Jesus to Peter. He said, "Let down your nets" (5:4). It's plural—*nets*. Peter answered, "I will let down the net [singular]" (5:5). As a result, "their net [singular] brake" (5:6). Peter understood the command but responded with partial obedience.

Despite Peter's half-hearted effort, Jesus graciously and abundantly blessed Peter.

I believe God desires to do the same for us. Consider this promise: "[He] is able to do exceeding abundantly above all that we ask or think, according to the power that worketh in us" (Ephesians 3:20). God can bless you in ways that you can't even imagine. God desires to overwhelm you with His blessing the way He did Peter and the disciples with fish. Only one thing can stop His blessing from being poured out on your life—disobedience. I missed out on the opportunity to experience a blessing (scoring a touchdown) that day many years ago because I refused to obey the clear directives of my coach. What is God asking you to do? Are you refusing to do it? Are you doing it halfway? Don't rob yourself of the abundant blessing of God by refusing to follow His clear directives.

### *DEPTH RESULTS IN HUMILITY*

If the story ended here, we might wrongly view the purpose of Jesus' blessing in a selfish way. We might conclude that the reason for blessing is so I can be blessed. We might view ourselves as the end of the blessing. However, God has a much larger purpose for blessing us abundantly. He does it to change our view of ourselves and, more importantly, to change our view of Him. "When Simon Peter saw it, he fell down at Jesus' knees, saying, Depart from me; for I am a sinful man, O Lord. [9]For he was astonished, and all that were with him, at the draught of the fishes which they had taken" (Luke 5:8–9). True depth results in humility. Peter went from being arrogant to being in astonished at Jesus. He became like a stone in the presence of Jesus. Peter's view of himself decreased while his opinion of Jesus increased. He fell at the feet of Jesus, recognizing Him as Lord, and declared himself to be a sinful man.

We see this same attitude demonstrated throughout Scripture but nowhere more clearly than in the life of John the Baptist when he declared that Jesus had to increase but he had to decrease (John 3:30). It's really a matter of finding our proper place before our Lord and Savior. We experience the same type of awe and astonishment toward King Jesus when we obediently follow through with His commandments and watch Him come through in miraculous ways. As He performs the unimaginable in our lives, we come to realize how truly amazing He is and how truly sinful we are. My opinion of myself sank, and my opinion of my coach grew as I watched his play calling work to perfection. Unfortunately, I had to observe this from the sideline because of my disobedience.

This happens to us way too often. We see God miraculously working in the life of His obedient followers as we sit on the sidelines of disobedience. We've been relegated to the bench because of our refusal to follow His very clear directives. God wants to use us and bless us, but because we lack willing and obedient hearts, He finds someone else who will carry out His play call. God doesn't stop working simply because *we* refuse to work for Him. Humble yourself under the mighty hand of God. Carry out His clear directives even when they go contrary to your will, and I promise you'll come to be astonished at the mighty workings of God in your life.

### *ABUNDANCE RESULTS IN ABANDON*

We tend to view the disciples as robotic when it came to following Jesus. He said come, and they came. He said go, and they went without question. What we fail to realize is that there were regular moments of surrender in the lives of the disciples. This is one of those moments. Notice how this story ends. "And so was also James, and John, the sons of Zebedee, which were partners with Simon. And Jesus said unto Simon, Fear not; from henceforth thou shalt catch men. And when they had brought their ships to land, they forsook all, and followed him" (Luke 5:10–11). Peter and his crew had not only come to recognize who Jesus was and to be in awe of Him, but they had made a decision to follow Him with abandonment. As soon as they got back to land, they forsook everything for the purpose of following Jesus. No longer did they allow the hindrances of life, including their own pride, to hold them back. No longer did they make excuses for why they couldn't follow Him wholeheartedly. They were all in.

After my disobedient episode on the football field and watching my teammates experience the abundance of a game-winning touchdown, I was a changed person. Never again did I question the play calls of my coach. I made a decision to wholeheartedly follow his every directive. The hindrances (my pride and fear) were gone. The excuses were put away. As a result, the coach's plan unfolded for our team, and we were really good. In the process I became a much better player than I ever was before.

It's no coincidence that the text specifically mentions the three disciples (Peter, James, and John) who are commonly referred to as Jesus' inner circle. At this point in their lives, these three men made a decision to forsake everything for the purpose of following Jesus. As a result, they were the three who experienced the deepest intimacy with Jesus and were exposed to things the other disciples didn't have the opportunity to witness. I believe the opportunities given to these three men had their origin in this moment. Their decision to leave all and follow him opened spiritual doors that few experience. Also, as a result of their decision to follow Jesus with abandon, Jesus shared their new purpose with them. He told them they were now going to be fishers of men. Their whole existence was now about following Jesus and catching souls. Don't miss this huge principle – revelation of purpose follows wholehearted obedience. God is not going to reveal the specific course for your life until you determine to follow Him regardless of where His course may lead you. We tend to get this part of spiritual life backwards. Our attitude is, "Show me what you want me to do, and if I like it, then I'll follow you with everything I've got." God desires for us to first obediently follow Him with abandon, and then He will reveal the specifics to us. Granted, this can be a little scary, but when we come to realize who Jesus really is, it makes the decision to follow Him much easier.

What's holding you back? What's keeping you from obediently serving Jesus with abandon? Is there a sin that is a continual source of stumbling for you? Are you hyper-focused on your career and upward mobility and therefore have little time for following Jesus? Are the relationships in your life toxic and keeping you from doing the right thing? Maybe you're just apathetic toward this whole God and Jesus thing. Maybe you're just afraid.

That last one seems to get us all from time to time. Fear grips our hearts and causes our spiritual lives to come to a screeching halt. Did you notice what Jesus said to Peter in the boat when he fell at His feet in astonishment? "Fear not" (Luke 5:10). Jesus was saying, "Peter, don't be afraid anymore. Follow Me and be a fisher of men." So much of what we do in life is driven by unfounded fear. Our drive to follow Jesus is halted by fear. Let's be honest. When we contemplate forsaking all and following Jesus with complete abandon, we get a little scared. Taking your life in a completely new direction without knowing what the Lord might ask of you can be an intimidating thing. He counsels us in the same manner He counseled Peter, "Fear not." Stand in awe of Him, and the fears of this life will diminish.

Let me ask you a similar question. What are you holding back from Jesus? In our story, Peter and the others forsook all and followed Jesus. Is there an area of your life that has been marked "off limits" to Jesus? Many people accept Jesus as the Savior of their souls but continue to deny Him access to certain sections of their lives. He can have our Sunday mornings, but not our 24/7 Monday through Friday. We want Him to attend our small group with us, but we won't allow Him to go along when we go out with our golfing buddies on Saturday morning. We'll give him a few minutes as we pray for a good day and ask a blessing on our food, but we won't let down our guard and allow His Spirit to pierce us with the Word of truth. Jesus isn't interested in this type of shallow, superficial relationship. He wants our following of Him to be with unmitigated abandon. What keeps us from having this type of all-in relationship with Jesus? Once again, it's our old enemy, fear. Mostly, it's our fear of losing control. We're fearful that Jesus will creep into every area of our lives and start wrecking things. We try to keep Him in the box we've created for Him because it's more comfortable that way.

But consider what happens when we work through our fear. When we allow God to fill us with courage and commit to following Him with abandon, His plan for our lives begins to come into focus. There's no shortage of advice in the Christian world today about God's purpose for us. By the time you read all the material, you may find yourself more confused than when you started. Let's keep this real simple. God's purpose for you is twofold: (1) follow Jesus and (2) fish for men. If you dedicate yourself to those two things, you'll be way ahead of the game. Most people get the "following Jesus" part of this equation, but what does it mean to be a "fisher of men"? Does it mean I have to be an evangelist or be one of those guys who stand on the street corner yelling "turn or burn" at people through a megaphone? No. To be a fisher of men is to be actively involved in the furtherance of God's kingdom through the spreading of His gospel. It's about helping others become followers who fish. That may involve you being an evangelist of sorts, or it may involve you serving in more of a supporting role within the church. The specific role will be determined by your specific gifting and calling. That's a different book for a different time. The point is that once we give ourselves over to obediently serving Him with abandon, the specifics of His plan for our lives and our involvement begin to come into focus.

There's little question that this event recorded in Luke 5 profoundly impacted those men. They were never the same from that moment forward. Sure they had times of setback and disappointment, but overall, I believe this was a benchmark moment for them that they continually came back to and thought about. At the very end of His earthly ministry, during some of the most confusing days of their lives, Jesus brings this event back to their memory once again. The events we are about to read were post-resurrection and pre-ascension. I think the disciples found themselves in limbo, trying to figure out what was going on. Not knowing what to do, Peter reverted back to his old way of life.

> Simon Peter saith unto them, I go a fishing. They say unto him, We also go with thee. They went forth, and entered into a ship immediately; and that night they caught nothing. But when the morning was now come, Jesus stood on the shore:

> but the disciples knew not that it was Jesus. Then Jesus saith unto them, Children, have ye any meat? They answered him, No. And he said unto them, Cast the net on the right side of the ship, and ye shall find. They cast therefore, and now they were not able to draw it for the multitude of fishes. Therefore that disciple whom Jesus loved saith unto Peter, It is the Lord. Now when Simon Peter heard that it was the Lord, he girt his fisher's coat unto him, (for he was naked,) and did cast himself into the sea. And the other disciples came in a little ship; (for they were not far from land, but as it were two hundred cubits,) dragging the net with fishes. (John 21:3–8)

This event and the one recorded in Luke are eerily similar. I guarantee you when Peter cast his net and caught all those fish, his mind immediately raced back to the day when he went deep with Jesus. He remembered he had committed to obediently following Jesus with abandon. He remembered the astonishment at the miracles this man could perform. He remembered he was no longer a commercial fisherman, but a fisher of men. After the trial and crucifixion, he had temporarily lost his way, but now he remembered what his life was all about—following Jesus and fishing for men. This calling on his life began with a commitment to obediently follow the clear commands of Jesus. God had given him an invitation to move out of the shallow waters and go deeper with Jesus. He accepted the invitation through his act of obedience, and life was never the same again.

We, like Peter, sometimes lose our way and need the Lord to remind us of our commitment to Him. We drift back into our former way of life, toiling with no meaningful results. If we're not careful, before we know it, we're standing in the shallow water near the shore once again and our relationship with God has become superficial at best. God is calling you back into the depths of a meaningful relationship with Him. He invites you to obediently cast your nets again and be blessed abundantly.

Sometimes when I feel my own life drifting back into the shallows, I think back to that fall day so long ago, and picture God in the huddle calling a quarterback sweep left. In that moment I am reminded that abundance and awe of God flow from obedience to His clear commands. This is true even when I don't fully understand the play call. Drifting back into the shallows of Christianity always results, first and foremost, from an unwillingness to follow His clear commands. If I want to hang out in the deep end of the pool with God, I've got to be willing to obey Him.

I want to finish this chapter with a simple and yet incredibly profound question, "What is God asking you to do?" Is He asking you to go left when you want to go right? Is He asking you to do something that goes contrary to everything you believe to be true? Is He asking you to obediently follow His commands when every fiber of your being says it's a colossal waste of time? What God is asking of you may scare you. It may not make sense to you. You may not really want to do it. But an unwillingness to obey will relegate you to a life in the spiritual kiddie pool, or worse yet, on the sidelines of life. God wants abandon, awe, and abundance to define your life, not restraint, fear, and superficiality. It's time for you to launch out into the deep. You do that by obediently following His clear commands for your life. Quarterback sweep left. On one. Ready break!

## YOUR LIFE PARABLE

1) The journey from shallowness to depth in your relationship with Jesus begins with your next step. What is the next step Jesus is asking you to take in your life—baptism, tithing, serving in ministry, witnessing to your friends and family? Chances are you know what your next step entails, and you simply need to take it. But if you don't know, seek counsel from your pastor about what God would have you do next.

2) The abundant Christian life results from following Jesus with abandon. Is there an area of your life where you think you know better than God? It's time to relinquish control and obediently follow the clear directives of your Lord.

3) What fear in your life is holding you back from following Jesus completely?

# 7

## The Fruit of Life

***Turning our worst moments into our best moments.***

Have you ever used the statement, "It's been one of those days"? How about, "It's been one of those weeks"? Take it a step further, "It's been one of those months!" We've all had times during life whether it was a day, week, or month when things weren't going exactly as planned, and it seemed the universe was conspiring against us. Maybe the difficulties were related to circumstances at work, relational issues at home, or a health concern for yourself or a loved one. Whatever the cause, we've all experienced those painful moments that cause us to look toward heaven and ask God, "Why in the world is this happening to me?"

For me 2012 was "one of those years." It was without question the least favorite of my forty-seven-plus years on this planet. At every turn it seemed I was getting hit with a new challenge that was larger than the last. It was the year from you-know-where. I'm not exaggerating when I say that I hated 2012. Frankly, it stunk! Let me take a moment and share some of the major events of 2012 that led to my disdain.

The year started on a high note as I traveled to India to do some missions work, but it quickly turned bad. In fact, while I was on that trip two things happened (one minor, one major) that started me down the rocky road of 2012. I was in southern India helping with a basketball clinic for about a hundred young people when I noticed my knee becoming progressively stiffer as the first day wore on. By the end of the second day my left knee was twice its normal size and moving around was laborious. An old injury had been aggravated by nearly thirty hours of air travel, coupled with two full days of demonstrating basketball drills. I have to admit, I was a little frustrated by the timing of my knee injury. After all, here I was doing the Lord's work, fulfilling the Great Commission, and suddenly my knee decides it's had enough. Couldn't the Lord have held this off a few more weeks? An MRI later revealed a torn meniscus and substantial arthritis in my knee. It would need to be repaired by arthroscopic surgery followed by several months of therapy. In the grand scope (get it?) of things my aching knee and subsequent surgery were relatively minor in comparison to the other horrible occurrences of 2012.

During that same trip to India, I received word via Skype that my father had been admitted to the hospital after becoming violently ill. It was discovered that he had a large growth in his abdomen that was blocking the bile duct and causing him to be very sick to his stomach. After a battery of tests, it was further discovered that his stomach region was filled with precancerous growths, and he would need a surgical procedure to remove not only the growths but a portion of his stomach, pancreas, gall bladder, and small intestine. My father had this surgery in the spring of 2012, and it didn't go well. There were several moments when I was certain he wouldn't make it and that I would never talk to my dad again this side of eternity. He spent three and a half months in intensive care as the medical staff did all they could to nurse him back to health. This was an incredibly difficult time for my family, especially my mom.

It's so hard to watch those you love experience pain. You hurt for them. The most difficult part for me was not being able to help more. I felt so helpless during this ordeal. At the time I lived twelve hundred miles away from my parents, and the periodic trips I took back to the Midwest and daily phone calls couldn't appease my desire to help Mom and Dad with the day-to-day struggles they were experiencing. Dad finally returned home from the hospital in July of 2012 and got much better and was able to enjoy a reasonable quality of life.

It wasn't only isolated occasional hardships that shaped my view of 2012. I also had the difficulty of navigating the day-to-day relational challenges associated with raising a teenager and a pre-teen. I love my kids dearly, and I am so proud of them in so many ways, but I think all parents would agree that parenting is the most difficult thing you'll ever do in life. At a time when it seemed like everything that could go wrong was, the intensity of parenting also seemed to go to new heights. Many of the issues were simply related to normal hormonal changes, which can cause unexplainable moodiness in even the most passive kid—teenage angst. We had boy/girl emotional issues. We had sibling rivalry—continual bickering that eventually becomes like fingernails on a chalkboard to the ears of any parent. We had out-and-out defiance. We even had to work through some heavier issues, which—for the sake of my kids—I will not discuss at this time.

It's safe to say that many nights our home didn't feel like the bright and cheery place we envisioned when we started our family. If I'm honest, I would have to admit that I was quite disgusted with how things were going in our home and how people were treating one another. There's no doubt that the stress associated with the other things going on during 2012 was a major contributing factor in some of this behavior and in my tainted view. However, that doesn't change the fact that the pain was real and the experience was not enjoyable. My wife and I had numerous tear-filled discussions while lying in bed at night. We took long walks as we talked and felt at a loss for what to do next. We prayed for countless hours, asking God to intervene in our situation. We did all we knew to do. We tried everything, but nothing was changing the situation for the better.

Coupled with all the other difficulties of 2012, I had the ever-present prospect that the church I was pastoring in central New Jersey might close at the end of the year. It was like a black cloud that darkened everything I did during the year. It didn't necessarily cause hardship, but it certainly intensified the difficult experiences of the year. Let me give you an overview of what was transpiring with the congregation. From an attendance standpoint the church was in decline and had been for the previous couple of years. While the level of giving was good for a church our size, the income wasn't sufficient to cover our day-to-day operation, and we had been funding the shortfall out of savings for almost five years.

As our board sat down to prepare the budget for 2012, we were faced with another year of decline and the prospect of making additional cuts to a budget that had already been cut to the bone. My opening comments set the tone for the board meeting that day. I told them I wasn't interested in another year of cuts where we tried to eke out an existence and survive another year. I wanted to go "all in" with our resources, time, and energy and see if God would bless us during 2012. We emerged from that meeting with four things we were going to pray about and use as an indication God wanted our church to continue beyond 2012. If God didn't want our church to continue beyond 2012, then we would take an unanswered prayer as indication He was closing this door. They were big prayer requests, but not too big for God.

During the course of the year our church prayed vigilantly for these things. (My leadership team met several times a week at 5:00 a.m. to pray that God would bless our church and answer our request). We served God like never before. We went "all in" with our resources and waited for God to bless. But heaven was silent! Our prayer wasn't answered—at least not the way we wanted it answered. As we entered the last quarter of the year, our church continued to struggle, and despair began to set in. Each week it became more difficult to remain upbeat and optimistic. I wrestled with what to say to our beloved congregation as we spent our last few weeks together. At the time, I was preaching through the Gospel of John, and my attention was drawn to the events of chapters thirteen through seventeen. These five chapters record Jesus' final instructions to His disciples before His crucifixion—the last things He wanted them to know as they faced the difficulty of His death and the fear of not having Him to guide them every day. I reasoned, "If it was good enough for Jesus and His disciples, then it will probably work for us." It was in the midst of these final days and through these final messages that God began to reshape my thinking with regard to the trials of 2012. He started to give me a very different perspective on the things I was facing.

As John 16 records, Jesus begins by telling His disciples they will face hardships after His departure. I appreciate this about Jesus. He doesn't sugarcoat it for His disciples. He tells them, "Even while you're following me, you will face great trials." He doesn't lead them to believe that following Him will result in life being grand and will cause all their problems to disappear. Paul tells us in 2 Timothy 3:12 that if we are living godly lives, we will suffer. He doesn't say "possibly," "maybe," or "most likely." He says it will happen. When you make the decision to follow Christ wholeheartedly and to live contrary to the values of the world, then you will suffer as a result.

This suffering can come from three possible sources. The first potential source of suffering is our flesh, or our old sin nature. When we decide to no longer live for the fulfillment of our fleshly desires, our sin nature has an all-out uprising. In Romans 7, Paul describes this turmoil as a war in his members between the "inward man" (new spiritual nature) and the "wretched man" (old sinful nature). Make no mistake about it, this is a battle for the ages. When you have lived your entire life for the satisfying of your flesh and then suddenly begin to live for the Lord, you're going to have a battle on your hands. It's going to be a struggle, and you're going to suffer through this fight.

The second potential source of suffering is our enemy, the devil. Our enemy won't stand idly by and watch us live for Jesus. As long as we're just going through the motions and making no significant impact with our life, the enemy will leave us alone and allow us to bask in our spiritual mediocrity. However, when we make the decision to become fully devoted followers of Jesus, he will rise up and withstand us. A heart fully directed to Christ will not go unchallenged by our enemy. Spiritual warfare is real (Ephesians 6:10–18), and as with any war, there is resulting suffering that occurs.

The third potential source of suffering is the world in general. The lifestyle promoted by Scripture is starkly countercultural. When we decide to no longer walk according to the course of this world (Ephesians 2:2), then we will come face to face with a societal majority moving a different direction. We will virtually be swimming upstream. The result of this countercultural lifestyle is often suffering. In some parts of the world, this can result in martyrdom, but in the Western world it's more likely to bring ridicule, contempt, and ostracism. Frequently, one result of living for Jesus in this world is suffering.

Jesus goes on to tell the disciples that as a result of hearing these words about experiencing trials, their hearts are filled with sorrow (John 16:6). What a perfect description of the flood of emotion that fills us up during times of hardship! Throughout 2012 there were times I felt like I was literally drowning. I was so overwhelmed with the situation, and I felt the floodwaters rising above my head. The poisonous waters of frustration, despair, discouragement, helplessness, anger, and hopelessness regularly flowed over my mouth and nose, and I began to choke on them.

It was during those times that God brought to remembrance a passage from the book of Psalms: "When my heart is overwhelmed: lead me to the rock that is higher than I" (61:2). It is in Christ that we find the firm footing necessary to remain standing in the floods of life. In those moments of overwhelming sorrow, we have a rock that lifts us up above our trials and gives us strength and stability. He is able to deliver us from those overwhelming emotions we all experience during times of intense pain. In John 16:7 Jesus makes a most unusual statement to His disciples; He says it is expedient, or advantageous, for them if He goes away and they are left alone. How could Jesus leaving and the disciples experiencing sorrow and suffering possibly be advantageous? The key is understanding that they aren't really alone. The reason He says this is because His departure was necessary in order for the Comforter to be sent to help them through this situation.

### *COMFORT IN TIMES OF SORROW*

The Comforter mentioned by Jesus in John 16 is none other than the Holy Spirit. One of His many functions is to comfort believers who find themselves in pain. It is God's Spirit who provides the comfort we need in the midst of sorrow. In times of suffering we seek comfort from many sources (friends, family, food, drugs, alcohol, or even running away), but no one and nothing can provide comfort like the Holy Spirit. Scripture plainly teaches that the Holy Spirit resides within all those who have placed their faith in Jesus Christ as Savior. It's God's Spirit who gives life to our soul and is the down payment from God that we have eternal life in Christ. Not only is the Holy Spirit active in our eternal life, He plays a huge role in our experiencing what John 10:10 refers to as an abundant life. As He comes to fill our lives and we become more in tune with His presence, we experience life to the full. God desires for us to be filled with His Spirit rather than with sorrow.

There were moments in 2012 when I wouldn't have made it had it not been for the comfort of God's Holy Spirit. There were days when I felt like I couldn't go on. There were moments when I found it hard to take my next breath. In those times He spoke into my heart and gave me the strength and courage to take the next step. It was the still, small voice of God's Spirit that enabled me to make it through life's most challenging moment. Cling to the promises of God. Take God at His Word when He tells you He will provide comfort in all your tribulation. "Blessed be God, even the Father of our Lord Jesus Christ, the Father of mercies, and the God of all comfort; who comforteth us in all our tribulation, that we may be able to comfort them which are in any trouble, by the comfort wherewith we ourselves are comforted of God" (2 Corinthians 1:3–4). God has promised to comfort us in *all* our tribulation and also wants to use that experience to enable us to comfort others who may be going through troubles in life. What a blessing to know that whatever comes my way, God will be there to comfort me in the midst of it and can take my pain and use it to minister to others in their times of struggle. But God wants to do more than simply help us get through our difficult times. God wants to do a greater work in our pain. He wants to take our pain and turn it into something new.

### *SORROW TURNED TO JOY*

Notice what Jesus says to His disciples as He continues: "Now Jesus knew that they were desirous to ask him, and said unto them, Do ye inquire among yourselves of that I said, A little while, and ye shall not see me: and again, a little while, and ye shall see me? Verily, verily, I say unto you, That ye shall weep and lament, but the world shall rejoice: and ye shall be sorrowful, but your sorrow shall be turned into joy. A woman when she is in travail hath sorrow, because her hour is come: but as soon as she is delivered of the child, she remembereth no more the anguish, for joy that a man is born into the world. And ye now therefore have sorrow: but I will see you again, and your heart shall rejoice, and your joy no man taketh from you" (John 16:19–22).

He promises them that they are about to experience sorrow as He departs for a little while. His disciples didn't know He was speaking of the sorrow they would experience at His crucifixion and subsequent burial. He promises them that in a little while they will see Him again and their sorrow will be turned into joy. This is obviously a reference to His resurrection. He was crucified, died, and was buried. But on the third day He rose again and made Himself known to His followers. I'm sure it was the longest three days of their entire lives—seventy-two hours filled with questions, doubt, loss, hopelessness, pain, grief, anger, unimaginable sorrow, and fear. However, their sorrow and fear was turned to joy and courage once the resurrected Lord appeared to them and gave them their marching orders. On the other side of their pain, they gained a godly perspective that allowed them to experience a joy that could not be taken away.

I appreciate the phrase Jesus uses several times in this passage—*a little while*. It reminds me that the pain I experience in this life is not permanent. It only lasts for *a little while*. Even a life filled with sorrow is but a vapor, a shadow, or a flowering plant when laid beside the scope of eternity. When we're in the middle of the struggle it seems anything but short in duration, but we trust that God will bring us through and in the process turn our sorrow into joy. Paul describes it this way: "For our light affliction, which is but for a moment, worketh for us a far more exceeding and eternal weight of glory" (2 Corinthians 4:17). The light affliction mentioned by Paul included beatings, imprisonment, starvation, shipwrecks, and persecution to name a few. He's able to call these afflictions "light" and "momentary" because he viewed them through the lenses of eternal perspective. He understood that God was doing a work in the midst of his pain and there would be eternal benefits that far outweighed the affliction he was experiencing for a little while.

At this point Jesus uses a metaphor that I believe is the key to maintaining the proper perspective on sorrow and other struggles in life. The metaphor Jesus chooses is that of a woman giving birth to a child: "A woman when she is in travail hath sorrow, because her hour is come: but as soon as she is delivered of the child, she remembereth no more the anguish" (John 16:21). When a woman is in the middle of labor, she is focused on only one thing—the pain. I've obviously never given birth to a child, but I am told that childbirth is one of the most excruciating types of pain one can experience. You'll get no argument from me! There's a reason God gave women the job of birthing children—they're tougher than men. Even the toughest of men (Navy-Seal-type tough) would wilt under the pain of giving birth. I go straight to bed when I get a tummy ache. I can't imagine enduring the birth process. When Jesus says a woman in travail (labor) has sorrow, we understand what He's saying. The woman is in intense pain, and she's considering nothing else but the pain. As we experience pain in life, we find it difficult to focus on anything else. The pain is a veil that is difficult for us to see through. Pain clouds our judgment and hampers our ability to look beyond the moment.

For me, all the events of 2012 were obscured by the pain I was experiencing. It tainted everything I did. Even the moments of happiness were dampened by a dark cloud of despair. What I was experiencing was always in the back of my mind. In the delivery room of life, there is no joy in labor, only pain. However, that all changes with the occurrence of one event.

Jesus says as soon as the child is delivered, the mother no longer remembers the anguish of birth but is filled with joy at the birth of her child. The moment the new mother holds that baby in her arms, all the pain fades away, and she's filled with immeasurable joy. All the discomfort leading up to that moment and all the pain of the delivery process pale in comparison to the joyfulness associated with holding that little baby in her arms. Her baby, the fruit of her womb, brings all things into perspective and turns her sorrow into joy—a joy that cannot be taken away. Don't miss this great truth! It's the fruit of your pain that turns sorrow into joy. In the heat of the moment, no one is overjoyed about having to endure pain. However, with time, perspective, and a little maturity, we will at some point be able to look back on our time of sorrow and see the spiritual fruit that grew out of that time. We see this principle taught beautifully in Hebrews 12:11: "Now no chastening for the present seemeth to be joyous, but grievous: nevertheless afterward it yieldeth the peaceable fruit of righteousness unto them which are exercised thereby." Again, in the moment there is no joy but only grief. Afterward, once we come through to the other side, we see the fruit of righteousness in our lives that which results from our being disciplined by God.

As I endured 2012, I had no joy. The pain clouded my ability to see what God was doing in my life, and I just wanted the pain to stop. But now, as I look back on all the events of 2012, I have an affection and joy in all the things that I went through. Don't get me wrong, the wounds still sting on occasion, but God has now given me a perspective that enables me to see the fruit that resulted from that time. That's why I can now say that 2012 was both the worst year of my life and the best year of my life. When the Lord finally turns your sorrow into joy, it's a joy that can never be taken away from you. From this point forward I will look back on that part of my life with great joy, knowing that the Lord did an unbelievable work in me during that time. That time of sorrow caused me to lean into the Lord and trust Him like never before. It created a bond between my Savior and me that can never be broken. Most of the happiness we experience is fleeting, but when the Lord takes our sorrow and turns it into true joy, that lasts forever. When this happens, you come to understand what the psalmist meant: "Thou hast turned for me my mourning into dancing: thou hast put off my sackcloth, and girded me with gladness" (Psalm 30:11). When the Lord does this work in your life, mourning becomes dancing, and grief is turned to gladness.

Maybe as you read this, you're in the middle of a great sorrow and can't even imagine looking at the current events of your life with joy and gladness. I totally understand that sentiment. However, based on the truth of God's Word and my own experience, I can assure you that one day your sorrow will be turned into a joy that can never be taken away from you. Stay the course because your sorrow is just for a little while. In this life we will have sorrow, but Jesus has overcome the world. The joy and glory we'll experience in eternity will make all our trials seem so small. In the middle of your sorrow, keep reminding yourself that the Lord is doing a great work in your life and that the pain is only temporary. Work hard to view your situation from an eternal perspective. If you continue to fight for the proper perspective, you'll find God's joy will begin to filter into your heart and start to overcome your sorrow.

### *PEACE IN TIMES OF TRIBULATION*

Jesus comforts us during our sorrow. Jesus takes our sorrow and turns it into joy. Jesus brings peace in the middle of tribulation: "Behold, the hour cometh, yea, is now come, that ye shall be scattered, every man to his own, and shall leave me alone: and yet I am not alone, because the Father is with me. These things I have spoken unto you, that in me ye might have peace. In the world ye shall have tribulation: but be of good cheer; I have overcome the world" (John 16:32–33). Jesus knew He was about to be abandoned by those who claimed to love Him most. The men He had spent the last three and a half years training were going to scatter like cockroaches when the lights come on. In the hour of His greatest need, those He loved the most wouldn't be there for Him. However, Jesus also knew that even though He would be by Himself, He would not be alone. His heavenly Father would be with Him throughout his ordeal. The Father's support didn't eliminate the struggle or alleviate the pain, but it gave Jesus the strength to endure. In the middle of His tribulation, He had peace knowing His Father was with Him. It was Jesus' intimate knowledge of the Father that gave Him the confidence that all would work out well in the end. He would overcome because His Father was Almighty God.

Going through trials and tribulations is a very lonely experience. You can be surrounded by friends, family, and acquaintances and yet feel all alone. You feel as though no one can relate to what you're experiencing. Your mind tricks you into believing that no one has ever been through what you are going through. It's during these times that we must remind ourselves that God is with us and that He will never leave us or forsake us (Hebrews 13:5). The knowledge that Immanuel is with us brings peace during times of trial. Notice where Jesus says peace is found: " These things I have spoken unto you, that *in me* ye might have peace" (John 16:33, emphasis added). As believers in Jesus Christ, we're said to be "in Christ" and therefore have access to God's incomprehensible peace. Through Jesus Christ we have "peace with God" (Romans 5:1). In our sinful state we were the enemies of God, but through the blood of Jesus Christ we have been reconciled to God. We have a peace treaty with God signed in the blood of Jesus. As a result of our "peace with God," we can experience the "peace of God" (Philippians 4:7). This is the kind of peace that rises above circumstances and prevails in the darkest moments of life. Though our world may be filled with tribulation and trials, we rest in His peace, knowing that He has overcome the world.

This world is not heaven, but we sometimes forget that very basic principle. We will undoubtedly experience tribulation during our lifetimes, but we can overcome because Jesus has overcome. Even believers whose lives end tragically will ultimately experience the victory and forever live in peace because they are "in Christ." Never forget that Jesus has already won the victory. Begin with His victory in mind, knowing that nothing will ever separate you from Him and His love. "As it is written, For thy sake we are killed all the day long; we are accounted as sheep for the slaughter. Nay, in all these things we are more than conquerors through him that loved us. For I am persuaded, that neither death, nor life, nor angels, nor principalities, nor powers, nor things present, nor things to come, nor height, nor depth, nor any other creature, shall be able to separate us from the love of God, which is in Christ Jesus our Lord" (Romans 8:36–39).

To the outside observer I'm sure my life in 2012 appeared to be tragic, meaningless, and unfair. I'm sure at times I appeared to be weak, defeated, and unsuccessful, especially as it related to the closing of the church in New Jersey. Strictly from a worldly standpoint, I couldn't blame someone for thinking that of me and coming to those conclusions. Through natural eyes I *was* weak and unsuccessful, and the events happening to me during 2012 *were* meaningless and unfair. However, God doesn't measure success the way we do, and times of tragedy are often used by God in the most powerful of ways. To know this is true, you need look no further than the cross of Calvary.

To the outside observer the events surrounding the crucifixion of Jesus were tragic, meaningless, and certainly unfair. Jesus Himself, no doubt, appeared to be weak and defeated as just another unsuccessful would-be messiah to the Jewish people. However, what no one understood then was that God was doing His greatest work through this seemingly tragic event. God turned this tragedy into the greatest harvest ever known. It's through the events surrounding Calvary that mankind is reconciled to God. From man's perspective it was tragic; from God's perspective, it was triumphant. That's why Isaiah 53:10 says that it "pleased the Lord to bruise him." God took pleasure in the crucifixion because He saw the fruit that would result from it. The event of the crucifixion was not pleasant for Jesus or His Father, but the knowledge of the long-term fruit gave them pleasure and joy. Jesus agonized over His impending crucifixion, but He was able to endure the cross because of the joy that would result.

"Looking unto Jesus the author and finisher of our faith; who for the joy that was set before him endured the cross, despising the shame, and is set down at the right hand of the throne of God. For consider him that endured such contradiction of sinners against himself, lest ye be wearied and faint in your minds" (Hebrews 12:2–3). Jesus understood His mission—the reconciliation of mankind to God. He knew that this mission would entail suffering and tribulation. He also understood the payoff would be worth whatever pain He had to endure. We look to Jesus as an example of enduring hardship while receiving comfort from the Father. Because of Jesus, we know our sorrow will be turned into joy and peace when we see the fruit associated with our labor.

At the beginning of this chapter, I told you I hated the year 2012. I said that it was the least favorite of all my years on this planet. However, just a few short years after the horrible events filling that year, I can honestly say that I now look back on that time with a great fondness. That's not to say that I don't still experience moments of sadness and regret when I reflect on that time in my life, but the overwhelming emotion associated with that time has been turned to joy. That joy flows from an understanding that God was doing a work in me during a time of great sorrow. I now see and understand that God used that time to bring forth fruit in my life. No one can ever take that away from me. These are lessons I will never forget.

I've come to realize life is about more than my personal comfort. It's about my character being molded into the likeness of Jesus. That molding process sometimes entails sorrow. But don't focus on the sorrow; focus on the fruit. I hope my story can bring you some hope in the midst of darkness. If you find yourself struggling right now through a time of great sorrow or tribulation, please know that God will comfort you. Cling to the hope that He will turn your sorrow to joy. Rest in the fact that He will give you a peace only He can provide. I know from personal experience that it is hard to see past the pain of the moment. Sometimes you feel it is all you can do to keep your head above water. You may hate what you're going through right now, but there's no doubt in my mind that God can turn that hatred into fondness. If you respond in the appropriate manner, you'll emerge from your crisis more fruitful—more like Jesus. And that's all any of us can ever hope for.

## YOUR LIFE PARABLE

1) What fruit do you see in your life as the direct result of experiencing a trial? Spend some time thanking God for this fruit and rejoicing in the work God has done in your life.

2) Is your heart filled with sorrow as you experience life's latest trial? Seek the Rock who is able to lift you above your circumstances and comfort your overwhelmed heart. Rest in the promise that God will comfort you and will one day turn your sorrow to joy.

3) Who do you know that's experiencing hardship right now? How would God have you to comfort them in the middle of their trials?

# 8

## The Giants of Life

***Overcoming our obstacles and entering the place of promise.***

Have you ever stared down a real-life giant? Known the sweet taste of victory associated with overcoming a seemingly insurmountable challenge? Or entered the place of blessedness God has prepared for all of His followers? You don't need me to tell you that life is filled with a myriad of giants, obstacles, and challenges. They cause us to cringe, cower, and sometimes even retreat. The giants of life block the pathway to the place where we can live solely based on the promises of God—a place where we can fulfill God's destiny for our lives. They stand like an impenetrable fortress stopping our progress to the Promised Land of God. In order to get there and become all that God desires for us to be, we must courageously face and overcome our giants. How do I know this? What gives me the assurance that our giants can be defeated? I've seen it happen. I've witnessed a real-life giant slayer in action and seen the victory that can come to those who, in spite of their fear, stand before the giant and allow God to bring them the victory.

When I say *giant slayer*, I'm sure your mind conjures up images of a six-foot-something knight in shining armor, built like Arnold Schwarzenegger (in his prime, before he was governor), with a square jaw, steely blue eyes, and a sword so big it would normally take two men to wield it. You know the type, a battle-tested soldier who wears the scars of battle like a badge of honor. The kind of warrior you would want on your side when a fight breaks out. However, the giant slayer I'm thinking of came in a slightly smaller package. He's about four feet tall, weighs sixty pounds soaking wet, and is only eight years old. His only scar came as a result of slipping on the doormat and hitting his head on the door hinge (requiring one stitch to close the wound). This genuine battle-tested giant slayer still sleeps with a "blanky" and a stuffed penguin named Waddle. He's my son, Drew, and while he may be a pint-sized warrior, his courage and valor far exceed the dimensions of his meager frame. He's my hero, and God has used this small but mighty slayer of giants to instruct his six-foot-six-inch dad about the art of giant warfare.

Drew's giant-slaying odyssey started about a year ago when my dear wife, in an effort to save me some time, scheduled simultaneous annual physicals for Drew and our five-year-old daughter, Abby. I thought, "Great, we'll get them both over with and be done. We're killing two birds with one stone. Very efficient. I love it!" The exams were going very well until the doctor announced they needed a TB test, blood work, and a flu shot! Uh oh! Did he just use the s- word? What started as a harmless, quick, and efficient outing to the pediatrician lapsed into what felt like forty years in the wilderness.

As soon as the doctor exited the room, the tears started to flow and the ear-piercing screaming commenced. Drew took up his position hiding under the exam table. His logic was sound—if you can't find me, you can't shoot me. My daughter, on the other hand, threw herself on the floor and had herself a full-fledged temper tantrum complete with kicking, screaming, crying, and even a little spitting. After a few rounds of WWF Smackdown wrestling, she ended up in my lap being held by me in a full Nelson (pun intended). Both kids screamed at a volume that brought the entire nursing staff running to help. They came in one by one, asking me if everything was all right and if they could help me in some way. I'm certain it wasn't the first time children had screamed and cried in their office because they were about to get shots, but I guarantee you, this was one for the ages. To this day when I visit the doctor, I see a smirk come over the nurses' faces as they reminisce about that day with the Nelson children—a day that shall forever live in infamy.

Finally, the nurse came in with her tray of needles and asked, "Who's first?" No one volunteered. Since I was already holding Abby, she was the lucky one. When she heard the good news, she went into full spider-monkey mode and started climbing me like a tree in the rainforest. It's truly amazing how strong a five-year-old girl can be when fear and adrenaline kick in. I finally corralled her and held her arm so that the nurse could administer the shot. The screams increased with every pinprick. Not only was Abby screaming because she was receiving the shot, but every time Abby screamed Drew let out an equally loud sympathy scream. It was like being trapped in a medieval torture chamber. You would have thought we were using thumbscrews on them or stretching them on the rack.

Eventually, we finished with Abby, and then I had to retrieve Drew from beneath the exam table. This was easier said than done as he had somehow managed to wedge himself between the wall and the table. I literally had to move the table to get him out. Second verse, same as the first. Fighting, screaming, climbing, sticking, crying, and finally sobbing. Needless to say, by the end of this ordeal, both kids were traumatized, and so was I. I was drenched with sweat and wanted to crawl under the exam table and have myself a good cry!

Human nature being what it is, I was looking for someone to blame. Though her intentions were good, my wife was going to hear about this when I got home. When I was done with her, she was going to want to crawl under a table and cry (just so you know, I'm all talk). I left the doctor's office that day carrying a sobbing child in each arm. The nurses and staff looked at us with sympathetic eyes but seemingly sadistic smirks. Life would never be the same. This tragic event left all of us indelibly marked.

As the next year wore on, my kids began to inquire about when they would once again have to visit the doctor for their annual checkup. They knew the last doctor's visit was around the beginning of school and so as school started, the frequency of their inquiries increased. About two weeks before the appointment, legitimate fear began to grip their little hearts. Each night as I tucked them in and asked what they would like to pray for, the subject of doctors and shots was at the top of the list. My son,

Drew, was especially frightened as the appointment date grew ever closer. Drew was going to meet his giant once again, and he wasn't looking forward to it! He wanted to run away; he wanted to avoid it. But in his heart he knew there was no other option but to face his foe head-on.

It's ironic, even divine, how these events transpired in my life. God was at work in my son's life, but He was also doing a major work in my life. Isn't it funny how that works? As I counseled Drew on how to best face his giant, God was counseling me on how to deal with the giants in my own life. God was using these circumstances to bring the truths of His Word to life. As I read a somewhat obscure story of two faithful Israeli spies in Numbers 13–14, God spoke to me and Drew regarding our giants. A passage of Scripture written thousands of years ago in a land far away was speaking directly to our situation with twenty-first-century giants. The Bible may be old, but its truths are timeless.

After returning from spying out the Promised Land, ten of the twelve spies deliver a solemn report and tell the people it's an incredible land, but the giant inhabitants are too tough. The spies return bearing the fruit of the land on their shoulders. The clusters of grapes are so large they must be carried on a staff between two men. They describe the land as flowing with milk and honey. This doesn't mean there are white streams of homogenized milk or rivers of golden honey winding through Canaan. Milk and honey is a metaphor for God's blessing, abundance, and fertility. The land is all God promised it would be and much more. This land is such a beautiful picture of the life we can have in Christ. God desires our life to abound with fruit (Galatians 5:22–23). God wants to give us a life of abundance (John 10:10). God wants to bless us beyond belief (Ephesians 1:3). The life God offers followers of Jesus exceeds our wildest expectations. It's what we've longed for our entire lives.

Despite how awesome the land is, the spies lead the people to believe there's no way they can overcome the obstacles it contains. They describe the inhabitants of the land as strong, very great giants who cover the entire land with massive walled cities. Their bottom-line message to the Israelites is that conquering this land will be incredibly hard and most likely impossible. It could take them years to drive out the inhabitants if they can even do it then. This is no cakewalk. Obviously the Israelites don't like hearing this message. They become discouraged and want to quit. The Israelites are like most of us—they want the payoff without the effort. They're looking for a quick easy fix to a major problem. They want the beach body without going to the gym. They want to lose fifty pounds but keep eating chips and cookie-dough ice cream. They want to be star athletes without practicing. Many Christians live in a type of fantasy world where they want to live like Jesus based on the promises of God but without doing battle with the giant obstacles in their lives. They want to live based on the promises of God, but they don't want to break a sweat in the process.

But two of the spies, Joshua and Caleb, go against the negative, pessimistic, and faithless opinion of their peers. They have a different message for the people. It's in their words that we find hope for facing our own giants. "If the Lord delight in us, then he will bring us into this land, and give it us; a land which floweth with milk and honey" (Numbers 14:8). God is for you. He delights in you. If you're a follower of Jesus, then you are God's child, and He desires the very best for you. He wants you to experience the abundant life so that you're living solely based on the promises of God. Notice that this verse says it is the Lord who will bring them into the land and give it to them. In other words, He's going to give them the ability to overcome the obstacles and give them the victory. Christ has overcome the world, and we have the victory in Him (John 16:33; 1 John 5:4; 1 Corinthians 15:57). The Promised Land of God lies before us. Despite the giant obstacles, it's ours for the taking. The question is "How do we battle the giants that are impeding our way into the place of abundance?"

### *FOCUS ON THE REWARD NOT THE GIANTS*

One thing you must know about my son, Drew, is that he is an absolute Lego freak! He would rather play with Legos than do anything else. He studies the catalog for hours on end, planning out what he wants for his birthday, Christmas, or the next time he has an extra fifty bucks lying around. My basement looks like a mini-Lego Land. I'm thinking about charging admission to all the people who want to go down and look at his latest creation. As Drew faced his giant, I made him an offer. I told him if he made it through this year's annual checkup and shot without screaming and hiding under the exam table, I would buy him the latest Star Wars Lego set. I know, that goes contrary to just about every wise parenting technique known to man, but I was desperate.

The morning of his appointment, Drew rolled out of bed without saying a word. He shuffled to the bathroom, eyes firmly fixed on his feet. He brushed his teeth, combed his hair, and got himself dressed for the day. His appointment wasn't until after school, so he had all day to think about his 3:00 p.m. rendezvous with a giant. After finally making his way downstairs, he sat at the kitchen table slumped over a bowl of Honey Nut Cheerios. I turned my attention away from making lunches and asked, "How long does a shot last?"

"I don't know," he said with tears welling up in his eyes, "and I'm not going."

I took his hand as we closed our eyes and counted together— one thousand one, one thousand two, one thousand three. "Done!" I said. "That's it! A shot only lasts for two to three seconds, and then it's over." I continued, "How long will you have fun playing with your new Lego set if you get through the shot without screaming?"

He shrugged.

"Hours and hours and hours," I said. Then I suggested, "Why don't you focus on the hours of fun you're going to have with your Lego set and not on the few seconds of pain from the shot?" His response was noncommittal, but he understood what I was getting at.

The Israelites who refused to enter the Promised Land were focused on the giants and their fear of battling them. They recognized the value of the reward (a good land filled with abundance and the prospect of much fruitfulness), but they couldn't get past the enormity of the giants in the land. Much of our attitude in life is driven by what we choose to focus on. Our thoughts (our focus) produce attitudes that result in actions (our way of living). Proverbs says it this way, "As he thinketh in his heart, so is he" (23:7). If your thoughts are continually negative, your attitude will be negative, and in turn, the resulting actions will not be good. The opposite is also true. If you focus your thoughts on positive things (Philippians 4:8), it will result in a good attitude, which in turn plays out in God-honoring actions. The Israelites' focus was too short-sighted: "The giants are big, and it will be hard." They needed to see the bigger picture. They needed to focus on the pay-off: "We and our children are going to enjoy the blessings of this land for generations to come."

When we focus on the giant or obstacle immediately in front of us, we're doomed to failure as well. We can learn from the mistake of the Israelites and focus on the reward that awaits us or the goal we're trying to achieve. We should concentrate on the way things will be once we get there and not on the giants standing in our way. Achieving this proper focus is really a matter of having the proper perspective on life and eternity. There's no doubt that God can give us victory and blessing during this lifetime. He can help us break free from a particular sin, overcome a lifelong habit, tear down a stronghold, and give us courage to move forward in spite of our fears. However, even if we never enjoy the blessings of overcoming giants during this lifetime, we must still keep our focus firmly fixed on the eternal payoff associated with engaging in the battle.

Paul tells us, "For I reckon that the sufferings of this present time are not worthy to be compared with the glory which shall be revealed in us" (Romans 8:18). There are eternal rewards in heaven that cannot be compared to the worst earthly suffering imaginable. Think of the worst possible earthly suffering; it can't compare to the reward that awaits those who faithfully serve the Lord. Think back to what I said to Drew about focusing on the hours of pleasure from playing with his new Lego set versus the few seconds of pain associated with the shot. How long will the pain from battling your giants last? One year, two years, three years, seventy years? How long will you enjoy the rewards of heaven? One millennia, two millennia, three millennia, infinity! Shift your focus from the temporary discomfort of facing your giants and onto the eternal joy associated with trusting God in the battle. Follow the advice Paul gives: "Look not at the things which are seen, but at the things which are not seen: for the things which are seen are temporal; but the things which are not seen are eternal" (2 Corinthians 4:18). All of us are guilty of continually underestimating the payoff of heaven. You may be a lifelong giant battler, but the bottom line is this—it will be more than worth it!

### *FOCUS ON THE LORD NOT YOURSELF*

Drew's pace slowed as we approached the doctor's office. I kneeled down beside him and tried to offer some words of encouragement. He looked at me with genuine fear in his eyes and said, "I don't know if I can do this." We made our way over to a bench just outside the doctor's office, sat down to talk and pray together. I told him that it's all right to be afraid and wonder if you were strong enough. It's in those moments that God is strong for us. When we are weak, He is strong on our behalf (2 Corinthians 12:7–10).

I asked Drew, "How big is God?"

His reply came quickly, "Huge!"

I continued, "Is there anything that God can't do?" Drew shook his head. "Well then, if God is huge, and there's nothing that He can't do, then why don't we think about Him and His power instead of thinking about ourselves and our weakness." We bowed our heads in prayer and asked God to give Drew the ability to be brave as he faced his giant. We were shifting our focus from our inability to God's ability.

The ten spies and other Israelites incorrectly evaluate their entry into the Promised Land only in terms of their strengths and abilities. "But the men that went up with him said, We be not able to go up against the people; for *they are stronger* than we. . . . And there we saw the giants, the sons of Anak, which come of the giants: and we were in our own sight as grasshoppers, and so we were in their sight" (Number 13:31, 33). Notice their view of themselves and their ability in comparison to the giants: "They are stronger," and we were "in our own sight as grasshoppers." When they compare their size and strength to that of the giants in the land, they feel like grasshoppers. Only one thing happens to grasshoppers when they come up against giants—they get squashed! In their estimation they don't have what it will take to get the job done. They're going to face a crushing defeat if they go up against these giants. They're forgetting one minor detail—God. Because they're focusing on the smallness of their own ability and not on the enormity of God, they're doomed to failure. Caleb tells the people, "If the Lord delight in us, then he will bring us into this land" (Numbers 14:8). He reminds them that God is the one who fights our battles for us. Caleb is attempting to shift the Israelites' focus from the problems and from self onto the Lord. His eyes are firmly fixed on the Lord because he knows that when our focus falls from the Lord to our circumstances, and to self, fear floods our heart.

We, like the Israelites, have a tendency to devalue ourselves, forget about God, and become hyper-focused on the giant circumstances and challenges we face in life. We become so consumed with the giants that we're unable to see who God is and what He's doing all around us. Let me see if I can bring this concept to life with a simple illustration. Let's say you're walking down the street and there happens to be a dime lying on the sidewalk. You aren't really paying attention and so you step on the dime and never really know it's there. In the same situation, if you did see the dime on the sidewalk, stopped, bent over, picked it up, and then held it front of your right eye while closing your left, what would happen? The dime would block out your entire view of the world. All you would be able to see would be the dime. Did the dime change? No, your focus changed. When we choose to focus on our circumstances, they block out everything else. When we choose to focus on the Lord, it allows us to keep our problems in their proper perspective and see all that God is doing around us. When our God is big, then our giants get smaller. When our giants grow in size, it's because our God has become small. In order to help us keep our focus on the enormity of our almighty God, let me end this section by giving you several passages of Scripture to think about and possibly memorize.

Isaiah 26:4 Trust ye in the Lord for ever: for in
the Lord Jehovah is everlasting strength.

Psalm 46:1 God is our refuge and strength,
a very present help in trouble.

Psalm 62:11 Power belongeth unto God.

Psalm 125:1 They that trust in the Lord shall be as mount
Zion, which cannot be removed, but abideth for ever.

Matthew 6:13 And lead us not into temptation,
but deliver us from evil: For thine is the kingdom,
and the power, and the glory, for ever. Amen.

Matthew 28:18 And Jesus came and spake unto them,
saying, All power is given unto me in heaven and in earth.

Philippians 4:13 I can do all things through
Christ which strengtheneth me.

Ephesians 3:16 That he would grant you, according
to the riches of his glory, to be strengthened
with might by his Spirit in the inner man.

Ephesians 6:10 Finally, my brethren, be strong
in the Lord, and in the power of his might.

### *DON'T BE AFRAID*

The time for battle had come. A giant stood before Drew in the guise of a two-inch needle on a stainless steel tray. Our hero was not clad in chain mail and armor, but in a blue gown with no back. Drew's bottom lip started to quiver as the nurse swabbed his arm with an alcohol-laced cotton ball. A huge tear rolled down one cheek, but not a single word passed his lips. As Drew faced his giant, he was undoubtedly afraid, but whereas the previous year he had crawled under the exam table to hide, this year he crawled on my lap and let me gently hold his arm. He closed his eyes and braced for the pain. I whispered in his ear, "It's OK. You're doing great! It's almost over. Daddy's here with you. I love you!"

In that moment, my own giants flashed through my mind as my heavenly Father whispered in my own heart: "It's OK. You're doing great! It's almost over. I'm with you. I love you." God's promises were coming to life for me. I suddenly had a greater appreciation for Hebrews 13:5, which says God will never leave me or forsake me. We're not alone even when we're by ourselves. I felt as though the promises of Isaiah 41:10 had been written directly to Drew and me: "Fear thou not; for I am with thee: be not dismayed; for I am thy God: I will strengthen thee; yea, I will help thee; yea, I will uphold thee with the right hand of my righteousness." We were being held in the right hand of God's righteousness as He held us, strengthened us, and helped us face our giants.

The primary reason the Israelites didn't enter the Promised Land is the same reason we fail to face the giants in our own lives—fear! "Only rebel not ye against the Lord, neither *fear* ye the people of the land; for they are bread for us: their defence is departed from them, and the Lord is with us: *fear* them not" (Numbers 14:9). We are fearful people. Phobias abound and keep us from achieving our desired destination in life. It's no coincidence that the most often repeated command in Scripture is "fear not." God knows we are fearful and is continually reminding us to not be afraid. In my experience I have observed that fear generally causes us to do one of two things—either we stop dead in our tracks and go no further, or we retreat from the place of blessing altogether. We either become paralyzed by fear, or we run away and hide. Obviously, these aren't the actions God desires to see displayed in His people, and so He offers another option—courage. Courage isn't the absence of fear; it's moving forward in spite of fear. Our courage comes from knowing that God is with us every step of the way. He has our backs, so to speak.

As Drew faced his giant, there were times when fear gripped him, and he wanted to run away and hide under an exam table. There were times when he felt the muscles in his entire body seize up so that he couldn't take another step. However, in Christ he found the strength to move forward in spite of his fear. He found courage in knowing his strength flowed from the Almighty. In the past, maybe you've fled or have been frozen before your giants. It's time for a change. It's time to find courage in Christ and to face your giants. Stand toe to toe with them, with the knowledge that God has your back. You can do this! It won't be easy, but nothing worthwhile ever is. If fear grips your heart, flee to the arms of your heavenly Father. Draw near and hear Him say, "It's OK. You're doing great! It's almost over. I'm with you. I love you."

### *YOU ARE GOING TO GROW!*

As the nurse finished up Drew's last shot and placed the "Snoopy" Band-aid on his left shoulder, he opened his eyes and said, "That's it! It's all over!" His arm was sore from the piercing giant attack, but the pain couldn't even compare to the joy he felt at having overcome his largest foe. While he got dressed, Drew proudly commented with a smile on his face, "I bet next year I don't even cry at all."

What happened to my son during his battle with the giant? He grew! Not in stature but in faith and the knowledge of God. As a result of battling this giant and trusting God through it, God was now more real to him. At the end of the day, the Christian life is about growth and transformation into the image of Jesus Christ. The apostle Peter tells us that we need to "grow in the grace and knowledge of our Lord and Savior" (2 Peter 3:18).

Often we have growing pains associated with increasing in our faith. Like most parents, my wife and I have tried just about every imaginable method of getting our kids to eat their vegetables. We've even stooped to pureeing them and putting them in brownies (I had to put a stop to that because it's just not right). Often you'd hear us reciting the standard parental line, "Eat your vegetables so you can grow big and strong like daddy." Now keep in mind that I am six-foot-six and tower over any five-year-old. One day my daughter looked at me with concern in her eyes after I had laid the "eat your veggies so you can be big like daddy" dictum on them. Her response to me was classic: "Daddy, you need to stop eating your veggies, or else you're going to be a giant!" She had given me a perfect excuse not to eat Brussels sprouts any more. At some point in life, we physically stop growing vertically (horizontally is a different story). But spiritually, we never stop growing. You can never get too big spiritually. Keep eating the meal God has prepared for you.

Joshua and Caleb offer a piece of parental advice that will help us understand the need to eat what God has prepared and our need for continual growth in our Christian life. It comes in the following unusual statement: "Only rebel not ye against the Lord, neither fear ye the people of the land; for they are bread for us" (Numbers 14:9). They're telling us that the giants we face and overcome in life are for our spiritual nourishment. While they may not taste the best, they are definitely good for you. They enable you to grow healthy and strong in your faith. The more you eat, the stronger you get and the better equipped you are to face even larger giants. Battling giants enables us to grow up big and strong like our heavenly Father.

God's menu sometimes includes feeding us with the bread of affliction. No one enjoys eating this type of bread, but we must understand that it causes us to draw closer to our heavenly Father. When we're faced with circumstances and situations beyond our control and strength, we must rely on Him to see us through. Peter tells us that during times of suffering, we should commit our souls to His keeping (1 Peter 4:19). Paul sought God's deliverance from his "thorn in the flesh" and when it didn't come as he had hoped, he found strength in his weakness. Paul came to realize that when he was weak, God's strength was on display through him (2 Corinthians 12:9–10). God offers us the same type of growth. He wants to help us eat the meal He has prepared for us. He'll cut it up in little pieces if He has to. Rely on Him, and He will get you through. When He does, your faith will increase.

God had mercy on me a few days later when my daughter went in for her annual check-up. Since Drew's appointment, the doctor had received a nasal mist flu vaccine to use in lieu of the standard shot. My daughter jumped at the option of having a little mist squirted up her nose versus a sharp object jammed into her flesh. Go figure! I was more than a little excited myself when I heard mist was an option. I was still worn out from helping Drew through his giant ordeal.

On the ride home that day, I was eager to see how Drew would respond to the news of his sister getting a mist instead of a shot. I knew she was going to needle him about it because that's what siblings do. I expected to hear the standard response of "it's not fair" from him, but his reaction truly floored me. He was actually happy for his sister but also proud that he had been able to overcome his own giant. He now stood on the other side of this ordeal with a resolve to trust God through tough situations. He was no longer afraid of this giant. While he didn't enjoy the pain of the shot, he wouldn't trade his experience for all the flu mists in the world. He wore his victory like a badge of honor and a reminder that with God's help we can make it through anything.

What giant are you currently standing toe to toe with—addiction, marital conflict, financial hardship, a rebellious child, habitual lying, relational turmoil, or an uncertain future? Everyone's giant is different, but we all face them. Battling the giants in our lives is not a pleasant thing. We don't go looking for these types of fights, but when they come our way, we must stand and fight. No one likes the pain associated with going through trials. If, however, we approach them with the proper focus—knowing that God is with us—we can emerge from battle having grown closer to our heavenly Father.

Hebrews 12:11 says it best: "Now no chastening for the present seemeth to be joyous, but grievous: nevertheless afterward it yieldeth the peaceable fruit of righteousness unto them which are exercised thereby." When you're in the middle of the battle, joy is elusive and grief is consuming. However, after the battle we gain a new perspective that results in peaceful and righteous fruit. On the other side of the battle, we can look back and see how God did a mighty work in and through us. Facing the giants of life, despite the pain, is good for us. Through the process we grow, and God becomes more real to us. Look past the giant that stands in front of you, and see the reward God has for you on the other side. Look past your own limitations, and see the strength of the Almighty who stands with you. Replace the fear that grips your heart with faith in your heavenly Father, who promises to never leave you or forsake you. Get ready to grow in the grace and knowledge of your Lord and Savior. God has giant things planned for you!

## YOUR LIFE PARABLES

1) What giant are you facing right now? What fear does your foe cause to grip your heart? What truth are you clinging to from God's Word to help you gain victory over your nemesis?

2) When facing the giants of life, your mindset is the key to victory. Remind yourself that the pain is temporary but the payoff is eternal. Fight the battle with an eternal perspective.

3) Memorize Philippians 4:13.

## Conclusion: Can You Hear Me Now?

***Preparing the soil of our heart to receive the seed of God's word.***

Hopefully, this book has given you some spiritual principles that can be of use in your walk with God. But more than that, I hope it has inspired you to begin communing with God in your own life. My prayer is that you would hear from God as you read His Word and see God at work in every circumstance of life. The stories in this book are my parables; the things God has shown me through the circumstances of my life. You have your own parables through which God is trying to communicate with you on a more meaningful basis. You can do more than just make it through life. You can begin experiencing God on a daily basis as the principles of His Word come alive in the ordinary affairs of your life. You can begin impacting the lives of others with the principles God has taught you in life. People need to hear your parables. However, before we can impact others we need to listen and pay attention to the life lessons of God. Let me conclude this book with one last parable from Jesus that will help us become more receptive to the Word of God in our lives.

I've often found myself in situations where I needed to hear from God. The reason behind my need varied from a need for direction, seeking answers, wanting proof, or an overwhelming desire to be changed by Him. God's responses to my desire to hear from Him have ranged from silence to abundance. At times it's as though heaven has opened up and God is speaking directly to me, and at other times, the sound of silence is almost deafening. What gives? Why do we sometimes hear from God, but other times heaven is silent? God is in the communication business. I personally believe He's continually attempting to communicate with mankind. If that's the case, why do we sometimes hear nothing? If God is always the same (a communicator) and His desire is always the same (to communicate), then the variable must lie within me. The variable is the condition of my heart. Frankly, there are times when my heart is not prepared to hear from God and so His communication falls on a deaf ear. The questions for us to consider are: "What causes our hearts to become unreceptive to the voice of God?" and "What can I do to prepare my heart to hear from Him?" Ironically, Jesus provides us with the answers to these questions in one of His most famous parables. It's found in Matthew 13.

Jesus looks at His audience and knows they're part of a primarily agrarian society. In order to teach them this important principle, He tells them a story about a sower (farmer), some seed, and four different types of soil. He mentions the wayside (a hard-packed path around the perimeter of the field), the stony place (soil filled with rocks that keep the roots of the plants from going deep), the thorny ground (where the weeds choke out the seed that is sown), and the good ground (where seed springs up and brings forth varying amounts of fruit).

In this parable, the sower represents God, the sower's seed typifies God's Word, and the four types of soil picture the varying conditions of the human heart. In the parable the sower is always the same. The seed that is being sown never changes. The variable in the story is the condition of the soil. Some ground is prepared to receive the seed and some is not. The causes of not hearing from God lie in the condition of this dirt. Let's examine each and see how we can begin living in the place of continual communion with God.

### *THE WAYSIDE (THE HARD HEART)*

"Hear ye therefore the parable of the sower. [19]When any one heareth the word of the kingdom, and understandeth it not, then cometh the wicked one, and catcheth away that which was sown in his heart. This is he which received seed by the way side" (Matthew 13:18–19). As I mentioned earlier, the wayside is the hard packed area around the perimeter of the field—the path the workers use to go around the field. You might have something similar in your yard if you have a dog that runs along a fence line or if there's a shortcut across the grass that gets a lot of pedestrian traffic. Over time, if left to itself, this dirt becomes so hard that it's like concrete, and there's no hope of anything growing in it because the seed is unable to penetrate the hard surface. Sadly, our hearts can become hardened toward God and His Word if we're not careful. We can become hardened to the point that we're closed to receiving God's Word. God is trying to speak into our lives but we've closed Him out and have allowed our hearts to become hard to His Word.

This type of hardness can be brought about by skepticism, preconceived ideas of how things are, past hurts, or the continual rejection of God's Word. Hardness typically happens over time. The human heart doesn't go from soft and receptive to rock-hard overnight. It usually takes years of being left unattended to get to the point of being hard-packed. Despite the hardened condition of the heart, God (the sower) is still trying to sow seed and get something to take root. God can grow plants in the hardest of places. I've seen trees growing out of rocks and literally splitting the rock in two. I've seen God's Word do miracles in the lives of people with the hardest of hearts.

Let me give a word of warning here. Maybe you're reading this and don't think the wayside heart applies to you because you consider yourself fairly receptive to the things of God. I believe it's possible for our hearts to be soft in certain areas but hard in others. Is there a particular area of your life (heart) that you've allowed to grow cold and hard toward God? This typically happens when we have something in our lives that we don't want to face or deal with. You can't leave those areas of hardness unattended because, over time, the resistance starts to creep into the other areas of your heart, and before you know it, you're unreceptive to any communication from God.

Soil that has hardened over time requires a good deal of work in order to make it receptive to seed once again. Each fall when I overseed my lawn with grass seed, I first spend some time turning over the hard soil in the bare spots so that it's more receptive to the sown seed. If I don't do the work of preparing the soil and breaking up the hard portions, it's unlikely any grass will grow in those spots. Once I've prepared the soil and sown the seed, I have to tend to the seed and soil by feeding it, and watering it; otherwise my efforts will be in vain. Left to itself the soil naturally moves back toward hardness. The soil of a hard heart must be broken up and turned over so that God can speak into it and bring forth fruit. This is easier said than done. It requires hard work and consistent attention. You have to work at keeping all areas of your heart soft and receptive to the things of God. You must continually search yourself and seek God's help in breaking up the clods in your heart.

When the seed of God's Word falls on a hardened heart, our enemy, the wicked one (the devil), swoops in and grabs the seed before it can take root in your life. The enemy will do everything in his power to keep God's seed from taking root in your life. You face a very real spiritual enemy who's trying keep God from speaking to you. The parable describes it as birds that come in and eat the seed before it can sprout. The enemy knows if he leaves the seed lying on your heart it stands a good chance of taking root. More than anything, your enemy desires to hinder your communication with God. If he can limit your ability to hear from God, he knows he will ultimately win the battle in your life. Don't give the enemy victory in your life by bringing a hardened heart to God. If you want to hear from God, you must bring Him a heart that's receptive to the seed of His Word.

### *STONY GROUND (THE SUPERFICIAL HEART)*

"But he that received the seed into stony places, the same is he that heareth the word, and anon with joy receiveth it; yet hath he not root in himself, but dureth for a while: for when tribulation or persecution ariseth because of the word, by and by he is offended" (Matthew 13:20–21).

Portions of Missouri, where I live, are some of the most fertile farmland anywhere in the United States. The land along the Missouri and Mississippi Rivers is black and rich, able to grow virtually any crop planted. In contrast the land of the Ozark Mountains in southern Missouri is red clay and filled with an abundance of rocks. My dad always said, "You pick up one rock, and you'll find five underneath it." Because of this rocky soil, it's very difficult to grow crops in southern Missouri. The plants can't put down deep enough roots to receive the nutrients they need to grow.

This is the second type of soil Jesus is describing. The seed is received with joy but can't endure very long because it doesn't have a deep root system. It is a soil filled with depth restrictors that keep everything on the surface. This soil represents someone who has become superficial in his relationship with God because his heart is filled with depth restrictors. A person who has a superficial relationship with God and His Word has no endurance when it comes to withstanding trials and persecutions or overcoming temptations. What is the primary depth restrictor in our hearts that keeps our relationship with God very shallow? You might answer this question in a number of different ways, but in my experience all depth restrictors originate in one common emotion—fear. We're afraid to go deep with God because of what He might ask us to do or what He might ask us to give up. We prefer to have a relationship with God that's the spiritual equivalent of talking about the weather rather than to go deep and have a relationship in which we regularly hear from God. God obviously wants us to go deep in our relationship with Him.

I love the way Paul says it: "For though I be absent in the flesh, yet am I with you in the spirit, joying and beholding your order, and the stedfastness of your faith in Christ. As ye have therefore received Christ Jesus the Lord, so walk ye in him: rooted and built up in him, and stablished in the faith, as ye have been taught, abounding therein with thanksgiving" (Colossians 2:6–7). We can't be built up until we first go deep with our roots. If you want to regularly hear from God, you're going to have to pull the rocks (depth restrictors) out of the soil of your heart. This is no easy task. In the same way pulling physical rocks from the soil is painstaking work, so too is removing the rocks from the soil of your heart. It requires a great deal of introspection and self-evaluation. It takes great diligence and perseverance because typically when you find one stone and remove it, there are five more underneath. As difficult as it may be to maintain a heart that is deep and receptive to God's Word, it's absolutely worth it. It is in the rock-free fertile soil that we find a profound relationship with God in which we continually commune with Him through His Word and develop a faith that's able to withstand the trials of life.

### *THORNY GROUND (THE DISTRACTED HEART)*

"He also that received seed among the thorns is he that heareth the word; and the care of this world, and the deceitfulness of riches, choke the word, and he becometh unfruitful" (Matthew 13:22).

Like most kids, when I was growing up, I had a set of chores I was responsible for around the house. Most of my chores were of the typical variety—mowing the grass, taking out the trash, and cleaning my room. I can't say that I necessarily liked doing my chores or that I never complained about having to do them. But for the most part they weren't too bad, and I didn't mind doing them with one major exception. Every summer my mom planted a huge garden in our backyard. She grew beans, cucumbers, tomatoes, corn, cantaloupe, watermelons, onions, carrots, and on and on and on. One of my annual summer chores was weeding the garden. I hated weeding that garden. Let me say that again more emphatically. I *hated* weeding the garden! It was hot, dirty, hard work with a payoff for me as a kid that was even worse—more vegetables to eat. Oh, boy! In hindsight I certainly understand the necessity and benefit of pulling weeds from a garden, but at the time I thought the weeds had just as much right to grow in the garden and should be left to themselves. May the best plant win! My mom knew what I didn't; in order to have a fruitful garden, you have pull the weeds, or else they will eventually choke out the good plants and overrun the garden.

The issue with the ground in this lies not with the quality of the soil but in the fact that it has two sets of plants growing in it. One set of plants is the fruit of the seed sown by God, and the other is thorns (weeds) that choke out what God is trying to do in this soil. For our purposes this soil represents a distracted or divided heart. This is a person who's trying to serve God and hear from God but who's also pursuing the things of the world. The passage describes the thorns as "the care of this world, and deceitfulness of riches." Luke 8:14 adds "pleasure" to the description. Here's the bottom line—you can't hope to hear from God consistently in your life while you have your heart set on pursuing the things of the world. We all think we're the exception to this rule, but none of us are. We cannot serve two masters and hope to have fruitful communion with God. The pull of the world is too strong and will eventually choke out what God is trying to do in our hearts. We see this in the example of Demas in 2 Timothy 4:10. Demas was a disciple of Christ who accompanied Paul on his missionary journeys, but at some point his love for the world grew so strong that it caused him to forsake Paul and the work of God.

God is trying to speak into the life of believers, but many have allowed their hearts to become so overgrown with the weeds of the world that God is unable to make a connection with them, and therefore, they never grow to maturity. Luke 8:14 tells us this ground could "bring no fruit to perfection." The word *perfection* means "completion or maturity." One of the major hindrances to believers coming to spiritual maturity is worldliness. They may have a form of godliness, but there's no power in it and certainly no meaningful communication from God. As followers of Jesus, we are to be strictly one-crop farmers. When we try to diversify and begin growing the crops of the world in the ground of our hearts, immediately the Word of God begins to die out as the worldly weeds choke it. If you want to hear from God on a consistent basis, then you've got to pull the worldly weeds out of your heart and allow the seed of God's Word to take root and bring forth mature fruit.

This is really a matter of priorities. We don't have to abandon all worldly possessions in order to hear from God, but He does need to be number one in your life. Many times we say God is the number-one priority of our lives, but our calendars, checkbooks, and involvement in ministry tell a different story. We need to make sure we're following the advice of Matthew 6:33 and seeking Him first in our life. Weeds grow quickly and quietly in a garden and require constant attention. The weeds of the world are equally as subtle as they creep into the garden of our hearts. Don't let the things of this world rob God of His rightful place on the throne of your heart and keep you from hearing from God.

### *GOOD GROUND (THE PREPARED HEART)*

"But he that received seed into the good ground is he that heareth the word, and understandeth it; which also beareth fruit, and bringeth forth, some an hundredfold, some sixty, some thirty" (Matthew 13:23).

The final piece of ground mentioned in Jesus' parable is the good ground that receives the seed and bears fruit. This soil typifies a person who hears the Word, understands the Word, and then allows the Word to bring forth fruit in his life. This is the type of heart that God desires us to have and that we should strive for. This is a heart that has been prepared to receive God's Word. The hard clods of the heart have been broken apart and become receptive to the seed of God's Word. The depth-restricting stones have been removed so the roots can go deep and get the nutrients necessary to withstand the trials of life. This ground is clear of worldly weeds, and the Word of God has free rein over the heart. What's the result of all this preparation? An abundance of mature fruit to the glory of God. In short, this is the purpose of mankind's existence. We are to glorify God, and the best way to do that is through a fruitful life.

Luke 8:15 adds that the fruit of the good ground is brought forth with patience (perseverance). Because of where we live and the time we live in, Christians often get impatient with the fruit-growing process. We want to hear from God *now*, and we want to experience the benefits of continual communion *immediately*. That's simply not how it works. All that is in our control is the condition of the soil. The fruit bearing and maturing process is in God's hands. No matter how much we fret or how impatient we become, we cannot make the fruit ripen more quickly. Growing to Christian maturity through continual communion in His Word doesn't happen overnight. In fact, it's a lifelong process. What we're discussing here isn't a quick-fix formula for hearing from God, but rather a process for a life filled with daily interactions with the Almighty, which in turn results in life-change.

Since God is continually seeking to communicate with mankind, He keeps sowing the seed of His Word into our hearts. The result depends on the condition of the soil. It seems foolish to me that the sower in the parable sows seed equally on each type of soil regardless of its condition. But this shows that God gives equal opportunity for everyone to receive His Word regardless of the condition of the hearts they bring to Him. What a gracious and merciful God we serve!

The seed is God's business and so is the fruit, but the condition of the soil is our business. When it comes to hearing from God, we're responsible for the receptivity of our hearts. Is His Word falling on a hardened heart, a stone-filled heart, or a thorn-infested heart as He tries to speak into your life? Or is the seed of His Word falling into the fertile soil of a heart prepared to commune with Him? These are questions only you can answer for yourself.

What steps can we take in order to prepare our hearts to hear from God? How can you begin to hear from God on a more consistent basis? How can we begin to sense God speaking to us through the everyday occurrences in our lives? Let me leave you with a few simple tips.

1) *Turn over the soil of your heart by humbling yourself before God.* Don't allow pride, skepticism, preconceived notions, or anything else to harden your heart toward God and His Word. Approach each day like a child eager to hear what God has to teach you. Begin to look at each experience in life as an opportunity to hear from God Almighty.
2) *Pull out the depth restrictors from your heart.* Let go of the fear that is keeping you from going deeper with God. God desires to have a deep, meaningful relationship with you. It's time for you to move past the superficial. It's time to get out of the baby pool and to jump head first into the deep end. Come on, take the plunge!

3) *Make God your priority on a daily basis.* Many Christians have experienced a moment in their lives when they surrendered to following God in a more meaningful way, only to slip back into a life of divided loyalties. I think this often happens because of a faulty way of viewing surrender. Surrendering to God and making Him your priority is not so much a moment-in-time decision as it is a moment-by-moment decision. Every single moment of every day has to be surrendered to Him as we ask ourselves, "Who's in charge in my life? God or me?" Every major decision has to be surrendered to Him. He has to be the priority in everything that we do throughout the day. This helps keep the world and its priorities from creeping into our hearts. When it comes to making God the priority of your life, you have to sweat the little stuff and follow Him even in the minutia of life.
4) *Be patient and persevere.* When you don't seem to be hearing from God and the fruit isn't coming as quickly as you'd like, hang in there and keep doing the right things in life. You can rest in the promise that if you give God a good heart, eventually His Word will bring forth fruit in your life. Don't give up too quickly and allow the soil of your heart to become a hard, rocky, or weed-infested place where God can't do any meaningful work.
5) *Listen for God's voice in the experiences of daily life.* Romans 1:20 tells us that His creation can instruct us about the deep things of God. Don't fall into the habit of just getting through life. Be still and know that He is God (Psalm 46:10). We often rush right by the lessons of God, trampling them as we hurry off to our next thing. God is speaking. God is instructing. God is telling a story. Become intentional about listening for the voice of God through the chaos of life.

www.ingramcontent.com/pod-product-compliance
Lightning Source LLC
Chambersburg PA
CBHW071858020426
42331CB00010B/2568

* 9 7 8 0 6 9 2 7 2 5 4 2 9 *